OCCASIONAL PAPER 139

Reinvigorating Growth in Developing Countries

Lessons from Adjustment Policies in Eight Economies

David Goldsbrough, Sharmini Coorey,
Louis Dicks-Mireaux, Balazs Horvath, Kalpana Kochhar,
Mauro Mecagni, Erik Offerdal, and Jianping Zhou

INTERNATIONAL MONETARY FUND
Washington DC
July 1996

© 1996 International Monetary Fund

Cataloging-in-Publication Data

Reinvigorating growth in developing countries: lessons from adjustment
policies in eight economies / David Goldsbrough . . . [et al.].
—Washington, D.C.: International Monetary Fund, 1996.
    p. cm. — (Occasional Paper, ISSN 0251-6365 ; no. 139)

    ISBN 1-55775-559-0

    1. Developing countries — Economic policy. 2. Saving and invest-
ment — Developing countries. 3. Labor market — Developing coun-
tries. 4. Loans, Foreign — Developing countries. I. Goldsbrough,
David John. II. Series: Occasional paper (International Monetary
Fund) ; no. 139.
HC597.R35   1996

Price: US$15.00
(US$12.00 to full-time faculty members and
students at universities and colleges)

Please send orders to:
International Monetary Fund, Publication Services
700 19th Street, N.W., Washington, D.C. 20431, U.S.A.
Tel.: (202) 623-7430   Telefax: (202) 623-7201
Internet: publications@imf.org

recycled paper

Contents

The following symbols have been used throughout this paper:

. . . to indicate that data are not available;

—   to indicate that the figure is zero or less than half the final digit shown, or that the item does not exist;

–   between years or months (e.g., 1991–92 or January–June) to indicate the years or months covered, including the beginning and ending years or months;

/   between years (e.g., 1991/92) to indicate a crop or fiscal (financial) year.

"Billion" means a thousand million.

Minor discrepancies between constituent figures and totals are due to rounding.

The term "country," as used in this paper, does not in all cases refer to a territorial entity that is a state as understood by international law and practice; the term also covers some territorial entities that are not states, but for which statistical data are maintained and provided internationally on a separate and independent basis.

Preface

This study examines the links between adjustment policies and growth in a small group of developing countries—Bangladesh, Chile, Ghana, India, Mexico, Morocco, Senegal, and Thailand—during 1970–93, reflecting information available through mid-1995. The study provides an overview of the adjustment and growth experience, examines in depth several policy issues of particular interest, and distills the principal policy lessons for the design of adjustment policies. The analysis builds on separate studies prepared for many of the countries in the context of the IMF's regular consultations with member countries, as well as on many other publications, articles, and work inside and outside the IMF and World Bank. A companion study, *Composition of Fiscal Adjustment and Growth* (forthcoming) examines issues related to the quality of fiscal adjustment.

The authors are indebted to numerous colleagues throughout the IMF for their assistance in the country analyses, in particular Rifaat Basanti, Elie Canetti, Ajai Chopra, Charles Collyns, Erik De Vrijer, Klaus Enders, Fernando Fernandez, Manal Fouad, Vicente Galbis, John Hicklin, Jianhai Lin, Michael Nowak, Karen Parker, Roohi Prem, Hugo Juan-Ramon, Marjorie Rose, Miguel Savastano, Amor Tahari, Van Can Thai, John Thornton, and Ewart Williams. They also thank Nadeem Haque, Peter Montiel, and Susan Schadler and many other colleagues in the Fund and World Bank for their valuable comments. They wish to thank Mehnaz Husain and Kadima Kalonji for research assistance and to Olivia Carolin and Fernanda Gusmao for secretarial support, and Esha Ray of the External Relations Department who edited the paper for publication and coordinated production. The opinions expressed in the paper are those of the authors and do not necessarily reflect the views of the IMF or of its Executive Directors.

I Introduction and Summary: Issues in Adjustment and Growth

Following the severe economic shocks—a sharp deterioration in the terms of trade and higher world interest rates—of the late 1970s and early 1980s and the ensuing debt crisis, a large number of developing countries undertook adjustment policies in order to restore growth on a sustainable basis. However, the medium-term response of growth and investment to these policies was frequently slow, even in countries that undertook significant measures. This study is born from that experience, and it aims to identify how adjustment policies could better contribute to reinvigorating growth in developing countries. The influence of macroeconomic policies and core structural reforms on the mainstays of growth—investment, saving, total factor productivity, and employment—is examined drawing upon the experience of eight developing countries. These are Bangladesh, Chile, Ghana, India, Mexico, Morocco, Senegal, and Thailand. The group was chosen to include both low- and middle-income cases as well as examples of countries that have, or have not, encountered external debt crises, and to include countries—most notably Chile and Thailand—that have achieved a markedly higher growth rate following a period of adjustment. The focus of this study is on policies and their effects rather than to estimate the independent effect of Fund-supported programs on growth. The analysis builds on separate studies prepared for many of the countries in the context of the IMF's regular consultations with member countries, known as Article IV consultations, as well as on many other books, articles, and work in the IMF and World Bank.[1] The main lessons emerging from studies other than this are summarized in Appendix I.

Methodology

The study uses a variety of methodological approaches, including growth accounting exercises, assessment of debt dynamics, and time-series regression analysis of private investment behavior, in addition to cross-country regressions contrasting the eight countries with a much larger sample. It also draws on other recent empirical work in the Fund on the determinants of national and private savings, and on work in the World Bank regarding structural reforms. The analysis is based on a case study approach, which offers a number of advantages, including the ability to examine the effects of policies in the context of complex economic and institutional settings that cannot be captured using cross-section studies. However, these benefits come at the expense of some inevitable questions about the generality of conclusions from a small sample of countries. The eight cases were chosen to reflect some geographic diversity and to include countries at different levels of development and different stages of adjustment, but the risks of sample selection bias cannot be excluded.

In view of the limited availability and quality of the data some potential methodological pitfalls with the approaches used in this study should be recognized. First, for some countries data constraints precluded sophisticated empirical techniques. Second, more elaborate approaches, such as estimating full structural models to assess the mix of stabilization policies and to generate counterfactual investment and growth scenarios, were not possible.[2] Third, even where econometric estimates are derived (for example, for investment), they may be biased if they do not take account of regime changes that alter how those policies influence the real economy. In practice, data limitations constrained the ability to correct for biases resulting from such regime changes;

---

[1]This work is referenced in the text and footnotes.

[2]In practice, no single model can capture all of the influences at work. One approach that attempts to generate "representative" estimates, from a panel of developing countries, for key macroeconomic parameters is described in Haque and others (1990) and Haque and Montiel (1991). Models with more complex production structures are needed to analyze many supply-side issues; data limitations prevent the estimation of such models for most developing countries, so a mixture of imposed and estimated parameters are typically used in simulations. This is the approach taken in Montiel (1993) and Bourguignon and Morrisson (1992). Also, see Khan and others (1991).

time series are too short, and the problems of identifying a stable policy reaction function in such circumstances are large. The study therefore relies upon a variety of partial evidence.

Economic growth can be measured in several ways. In particular, one must distinguish between national income and domestic product by taking account of the need to service any external borrowing. Growth in GNP or GNP per capita may be a better indicator of welfare, but for a number of countries in the study consistent time series of sufficient length are only available for GDP. Growth can also be measured at domestic or international relative prices. Since growth at domestic prices is how the effects of policies are usually assessed, it is the measure used for most of the study. For most countries, it does not make much difference which set of relative prices is used, but there are a few exceptions, especially for countries undergoing a transition from highly distorted trade regimes (see Appendix II, section on Long-Term Cross-Country Comparisons).

Summary of Findings

Crisis, Adjustment, and Growth

The adjustment episodes in each country were typically triggered by large financial imbalances or extensive structural problems or both. Most of the countries had suffered adverse external shocks that typically interacted with an inadequate policy response and heavy external borrowing to precipitate a crisis and a severe external financing constraint.

The *short-term response* to adjustment policies differed: output and investment declined severely in Chile and Mexico and modestly in India, Morocco, Senegal, and Thailand; there was no immediate impact on output and investment in Bangladesh. In Ghana, growth picked up quickly as the external financing constraint was reversed. The *medium-term growth response* also differed considerably. Simple time-series comparisons as well as the results of panel regressions based on a control-group approach suggest that Chile, Thailand, and to a lesser extent Ghana, shifted to a higher growth path following the implementation of adjustment policies. In Chile and Thailand, this outcome was supported by large and sustained increases in private investment and domestic saving, as well as capital inflows. The investment and growth response in India and Morocco was more muted and in Senegal was weak; Bangladesh showed no marked shift toward a higher growth path. In Mexico the recovery in investment was eventually quite significant but did not translate in

substantially higher rates of recorded output. This performance was perplexing in light of the progress toward macroeconomic stability and structural reform.[3]

How Can Adjustment Policies Foster Growth?

The links between growth and economic policies—both in the macroeconomic and structural areas—are complex and do not lend themselves easily to empirical analysis. Nevertheless, cross-country regressions using a large sample of countries suggest that growth, investment, and productivity developments are negatively correlated with *macroeconomic instability, structural distortions,* and *adverse terms of trade movements.* Shifts over time in the growth performance of the eight countries are examined in control-group regressions that take account of physical and human capital accumulation, differences in initial income levels, exogenous factors such as the terms of trade, as well as macroeconomic policies. The analysis suggests that countries that experienced especially severe episodes of macroeconomic instability, including very high inflation (Chile, Ghana, and Mexico), had growth rates well below the world average during these episodes. Although other exogenous factors may influence both growth and other macroeconomic indicators, making it difficult to identify the direction of causation, the results do reinforce the judgment that macroeconomic instability has generally been associated with an adverse impact on growth. In contrast, the confidence generated by a track record of stable, nondistortionary economic policies appears to have been important in generating a growth rate in Thailand consistently above the world average.

An inappropriate design of adjustment policies may prolong macroeconomic instability and uncertainty and thus sap private confidence. The experience of the eight countries points to three crucial aspects of policies: *timeliness, sustainability,* and *consistency.* Delaying adjustment invites a crisis environment that results in a necessarily abrupt contraction of domestic absorption. This contraction typically fell heavily on investment—public and private—and often gave little time for resources to switch toward the tradable goods sector. This appears to have been due partly to a rational "wait and see" attitude among private investors when faced with increased uncertainty and partly to ad hoc crisis measures that reduced confidence. Promoting more rapid resource switching and reducing the lags in the

---

[3]This study does not address explicitly the causes of the 1994 Mexican financial crisis.

response of private investors require the implementation of mutually consistent policies, an integral component of which is a medium-term fiscal position that is sustainable. Considerable progress toward fiscal sustainability was achieved in many countries, most notably in Chile, Mexico, Morocco, and Thailand, according to a relatively narrow public-debt-stability criterion. Yet this gauge of sustainability does not necessarily ensure that fiscal policy is consistent with objectives for growth and the external position, because of possible unpredictable shifts in private saving and investment behavior in response to comprehensive macroeconomic and structural adjustment.

The Response of Investment and Saving

Theory suggests that a *"pause" in private investment* may be a rational response to adjustment policies if relative prices are highly uncertain and policies are poorly coordinated and likely to be reversed. A number of countries in the group experienced such a pause, which in several cases lasted two–four years before private investment began to respond to improved macroeconomic balances and structural reform measures. Econometric evidence of investment behavior indicates that—in addition to "conventional" factors such as past growth of economic activity, real interest rates, and private sector credit—private investment was significantly influenced by uncertainty and macroeconomic instability. Indeed, during episodes of macroeconomic instability, private investment generally declined more than could be predicted on the basis of these investment equations. Also, a comparison of program targets with actual outcomes suggests that, on average, targets under Fund-supported programs in the eight countries were generally too sanguine about the prospects for an early rebound in private investment.

The largest and most lasting increases in *saving* were achieved in Chile and Thailand, suggesting that in these two countries higher saving and growth were mutually reinforcing over the medium term. Other countries had a more muted response. As has also been suggested by a number of other studies, the most important policy influence on overall saving appears to have been changes in the level of public saving; however, a history of macroeconomic stability was also important in Thailand, and public sector reforms (of the tax, public enterprise, and pension systems) appear to have contributed to boosting saving in Chile.

Robust empirical links between *external financing* and growth cannot be easily identified, since economic policies influence both in complex ways. When imports had been severely compressed due to

a balance of payments crisis, renewed access to external financing appears to have contributed to a rebound in growth (Ghana and India). Also, for those countries, such as Mexico, that experienced major debt-servicing difficulties, the debt crisis and its resolution had important indirect effects on investment and growth through their impact on confidence, interest rates, and the availability of credit to the private sector. More generally, the eight countries support the view that a timely availability of additional financing is likely to enhance growth prospects provided that supporting policies are in place: over the medium term, countries with favorable structural policies and improved public saving were the most successful in attracting capital inflows and channeling them toward increased investment.

Structural Reforms and Labor Markets

While it is a widely accepted notion that *structural reforms* enhance growth by improving the efficiency of resource allocation and expanding the productive capacity of the economy, rigorous empirical support for the links between reforms and productivity growth is difficult to establish. However, the experience of the eight countries suggests that those that began with relatively small structural distortions (Thailand) or made significant progress toward eliminating major distortions (Chile and Ghana) tended to experience the most rapid productivity gains, whereas those that made little progress with structural reform (Senegal) tended to have sluggish productivity growth. Although the country studies suggest that commonly identified "best practices" in structural reform in the trade and financial areas were not always associated with the strongest supply responses, they do support the view that in each country there are often strong complementarities between certain key reforms. The precise nature of these critical links varied from country to country, so there is no single blueprint on an appropriate sequencing of reforms.

With the exception of Thailand, all of the countries had considerable initial *labor market* rigidities (sometimes including extensive market segmentation or wage indexation or both) that impeded real wage flexibility. These features remained largely unchanged during the adjustment process; only Chile implemented significant reforms. Empirical evidence from the eight countries, albeit patchy, suggests that real wage flexibility was an important influence on the elasticity of employment with respect to output whereas failure to address backward-looking wage indexation was likely to exacerbate the negative effects on output and employment during disinflation episodes.

Key Lessons for the Design of IMF-Supported Programs

The key lessons for program design that emerge from the country studies are summarized here and are discussed in more detail in Section X.

• *Delayed adjustment is costly.* Stabilization policies undertaken in the context of a macroeconomic crisis will generally have deeper contractionary effects than policies implemented in a more timely manner. Two lessons arise for IMF operations. First, as an economy emerges from such a crisis, there are limits to what adjustment policies can, and should be expected to, achieve for investment and growth in the short term. Second, the role of effective surveillance is central to improving growth prospects—through detecting imbalances at an early stage and encouraging timely policies to address them.

• *A forward-looking medium-term framework is essential.* The sustainability and consistency of policies are central to preventing an economy from being locked into a low-investment, low-growth equilibrium. In a number of cases, inconsistencies between different components of the adjustment effort (for example, between exchange rate, fiscal, and wage policies; or between the goals of fiscal consolidation and certain structural reforms) appear to have weakened the supply response and sometimes led to policy reversals. Furthermore, private saving and investment decisions are essentially forward-looking in nature and can be heavily influenced by expectational and confidence factors. Greater emphasis should therefore be placed on conducting program reviews and postprogram surveillance within a consistent, medium-term macroeconomic framework. When investment and saving deviate significantly from program targets, policies should be revamped in the context of this framework in order to increase the prospects for achieving the authorities' growth and external objectives.

• *The fiscal position is critical.* Fiscal adjustment should be strong enough both to minimize the adverse effects on private investment through the impact on interest rates and the availability of credit to the private sector, and to support real exchange rate adjustment to promote resource switching and thereby minimize the initial output contraction. To this end, program design should address as explicitly as possible: (1) the assumed links between credit availability, interest rates, and private investment; (2) the problems of weak bank portfolios; and (3) the sustainability of the fiscal position in a medium-term framework.

• *Increasing public saving is likely to be the most effective means of raising national saving in the short run.* Nevertheless, a partial offset in private saving typically should be expected. Program projections for private saving should take careful account of this offset as well as the empirical evidence on the determinants of saving in each country.

• *Structural reform: the need for an early start and a critical mass.* In each country case strong complementarities between the effects of certain structural reforms were apparent, suggesting that carefully combining mutually supportive reforms is likely to maximize the beneficial impact on growth. Program design should emphasize early technical preparation and implementation of these reforms. Moreover, insufficient emphasis on, or delays in, implementing sectoral-level measures can dampen the supply response to macro-level reforms. Both these factors underscore the importance of close coordination with the World Bank in identifying and monitoring the "core" reforms in each country.

• *Is there a blueprint for achieving a transition to faster growth?* The linkages between policies and growth are often indirect, and many factors other than policies may have an impact on growth. Nonetheless, Chile and Thailand—two countries with very different economic histories—both appear to have achieved a transition to a more rapid growth path and to have had a number of common elements in the policies they implemented: a set of macroeconomic policies that were internally consistent and sustainable and that provided adequate incentives for the tradable goods sector; structural reforms that were successful in establishing the private sector as the main engine of growth; relatively flexible labor markets; and policies that helped direct external capital inflows toward investment rather than consumption.

* * *

The study is organized as follows. Section II begins with a summary of long-term trends in growth and investment, then briefly describes the episodes of adjustment: the initial conditions and external environment in which adjustment was initiated and the subsequent growth response. The next seven sections examine in depth several policy issues of particular interest, supported by five technical appendices. Section III discusses the evidence from cross-country econometric work on factors influencing long-term growth. Section IV examines the role of macroeconomic policies. Factors explaining the path of private investment and saving are discussed in Sections V and VI, respectively, and Section VII explores the role of external financing; Section VIII examines structural reforms; and Section IX discusses labor markets. The final section sets out specific policy conclusions and lessons for the design of adjustment policies.

II Overview of Adjustment

Under the IMF's mandate, resolving member countries' external financing problems must receive priority in IMF-supported programs; this objective, however, should be pursued with sensitivity toward the ultimate goal of economic policies, namely, improving living standards through higher growth. This was an important message of the last review of the conditionality attached to the use of IMF resources.[4] The review found that although, on average, growth strengthened moderately over the period covered, no country shifted to a distinctly more rapid pace of growth.

With this background, the present study investigates further the links between adjustment policies and growth by examining, from a medium-term perspective, how macroeconomic policies and core structural reforms—not all of which were implemented in the context of IMF-supported programs—have influenced the investment, saving, and employment performance of the eight countries.[5] A companion study, *Composition of Fiscal Adjustment and Growth*, examines issues related to the quality of fiscal adjustment in these countries, including the extent to which fiscal adjustment was undertaken in a manner that maintained expenditures with high social rates of return and implemented a growth-oriented tax system.[6] A brief overview of key developments in each country is given in Box 1.

The central question to be addressed is why, even in countries that took strong measures, the response of investment and growth has sometimes been slow.[7] In attempting to answer this question, one must bear in mind that adjustment policies had to be designed and implemented to take account of many constraints, including those imposed by the political process and administrative capacity.[8]

Adjustment policies can influence growth by affecting the degree of capacity utilization, the pace at which factor inputs are accumulated, and the efficiency with which those factors are used. The natural framework for considering these influences is through a combination of a growth model—in which the expansion of potential output is determined by increases in labor supply, physical and human capital, as well as improvements in productivity—and an open economy macroeconomic model, where changes in aggregate demand influence capacity utilization. The main links between the two components of this framework are saving and investment, which influence both the level of aggregate demand and the expansion in potential output. Consequently, the major focus of the study is on how adjustment policies influence growth through these two variables and through changes in total factor productivity.

An adjustment program generally includes a combination of stabilization measures and structural reforms. The former aim at restoring macroeconomic balance by bringing the level of demand and its composition (that is, tradable relative to nontradable goods) into line with output capacity and a sustainable external current account position. The latter comprise microeconomic and institutional reforms directed at fostering an efficient allocation of resources and removing obstacles to saving and investment. The effects of both types of policies are closely interlinked and are likely to have both short- and long-term consequences. On the one hand, the mix of macroeconomic policies affects long-term growth through its effects on saving and investment.

---

[4]See Schadler and others (1995) and Schadler (1995).

[5]The role of macroeconomic policies and reforms in growth has been the subject of many studies—see Appendix I. An early contribution on the role of IMF-supported adjustment programs is Khan and Knight (1985).

[6]Mackenzie and others (forthcoming).

[7]For this reason, no countries were included in which adjustment policies were especially weak. Nor are the transition economies represented, since their growth performance has been subject to a number of quite different influences.

[8]Asilis and Milesi-Ferreti (1994) provide a survey of (typically highly stylized) studies of how initial economic conditions, institutions, and political systems may interact with policy choices to influence the political sustainability of reforms. Uncertainty and conflict over the distributional consequences of adjustment generally play a key role in explaining delays in implementing stabilization in such models, suggesting that adjustment is more likely to be delayed the more polarized the society.

Box 1. An Overview of Adjustment in the Eight Countries

Bangladesh

After an extended period in the 1970s of political turmoil, heavy government intervention in the economy, and poor growth performance, the Government initiated an ambitious growth-oriented strategy in 1979. This strategy targeted increased saving and investment combined with extensive structural reforms; in the event, these targets were missed by wide margins on account of adverse shocks and policy slippages, so that macroeconomic imbalances continued to increase. A second phase of adjustment started in the mid-1980s; the combination of fiscal tightening and structural reforms, in particular unification of the foreign exchange market and trade liberalization, succeeded in reducing inflation and improving the external current account. Real per capita GDP growth remained low, however, in part because of continuing serious structural distortions.

Chile

A large drop in output in 1973 accompanied by hyperinflation led to the adoption of an economic program in 1974–75 involving a sharp tightening of fiscal policy, large corrective price increases, a flexible exchange rate policy, and significant structural reforms including a reversal of the previous expropriation of enterprises. Aiming to reduce inflation to world levels, the authorities fixed the exchange rate in mid-1979, but the inconsistency of this policy with wage indexation and ongoing inflation in nontradables led to a sharp real effective appreciation of the peso and a boom in consumption and imports financed by large external borrowing, accompanied by lax control of banking activity. A drop in the price of copper and an abrupt decline in access to external financing in the wake of the debt crisis led to a severe recession and a banking crisis in 1982–83. The medium-term stabilization and adjustment program adopted in 1983 included a flexible exchange rate, eliminating mandatory wage indexation,

restoring the financial system, and reducing the fiscal deficit. Further privatization of public enterprises was carried out and there was a major reform of the social security system. Since 1985 Chile has enjoyed strong economic growth.

Ghana

The Economic Recovery Program introduced in 1983 followed a protracted period of economic decline caused by massively interventionist policies, widespread price controls and exchange restrictions, and a large decline in the terms of trade. The first phase of the program (1983–86) was based on restrained financial policies, elimination of widespread domestic price controls and other regulatory restrictions, and large devaluations to correct a severely overvalued exchange rate—succeeded in eliminating the most severe macroeconomic imbalances. At the same time, a resumption of official external financing supported a pickup in public investment. The second phase (1987–91) completed the comprehensive liberalization of the trade and exchange system and featured a reform of the financial system as well as more vigorous efforts to restructure and privatize a large public enterprise sector.

India

In the second half of the 1980s, expansionary fiscal policies, including stepped-up public investment, brought about some pickup in growth, but also contributed to wider external current account deficits and rising external debt. Shocks to the balance of payments, associated with the 1990 Middle East crisis, and internal political problems triggered an outflow of capital and a major liquidity crisis in early 1991. A new government responded by depreciating the rupee, raising interest rates, cutting the public sector deficit, and implementing significant, but incomplete, structural reforms—most notably industrial deregulation, partial

---

On the other hand, structural reforms can have major consequences for macroeconomic stability. Transformation of tax and expenditure systems is often the keystone to sustainable fiscal adjustment, and financial, external, and labor market reforms can all influence how an economy responds to stabilization measures.

One additional feature of this broad framework is of particular importance to the discussion in this study: since investment and saving are inherently forward-looking decisions, they are heavily influenced by expectations about the future course of policies. Therefore, the effects of policies on private investment and saving can depend crucially on the

degree to which they are judged to be consistent and are expected to be sustained. For such reasons the last review of IMF conditionality emphasized that programs would benefit from being set in a medium-term context, with more focus on what constitutes a sustainable fiscal policy from both a financial and structural viewpoint.[9]

To help organize the discussion, specific "adjustment periods" for each country are used in certain sections of the study. The choice of such periods is somewhat arbitrary, especially since adjustment can

---

[9]Schadler and others (1995).

trade liberalization, and an opening up to foreign investment. In response, the balance of payments position strengthened substantially during 1992–94, aided by capital inflows.

Mexico

After the 1982 debt crisis and a cutoff from external financing, Mexico introduced an adjustment strategy based on fiscal tightening, frequent adjustments of the exchange rate, some moderate privatization, and after 1985, trade liberalization. Inflation remained high, however, while growth and private investment stagnated. A new disinflation strategy, introduced in December 1987, was based on further fiscal tightening, and the use of the exchange rate as the main nominal anchor supported by incomes policy agreements among labor, business and the government. Together with a successful restructuring of external debt, this strategy slowed inflation and paved the way for a resumption of access to international financial markets, and a surge of capital inflows. However, the real exchange rate appreciated, private saving declined sharply, and a large external current account deficit emerged, leading eventually to a new crisis in late 1994.

Morocco

During the 1970s, expansionary financial policies—prompted by the 1974 phosphate boom—resulted in large fiscal and external current account deficits and a rapid buildup of external debt. These imbalances added to a wide range of structural weaknesses. A succession of adverse exogenous shocks critically weakened the external position, leading to debt-servicing difficulties by the early 1980s. The subsequent adjustment strategy had several phases: through 1985, the emphasis was on fiscal adjustment by means of large cuts in capital expenditure (with most of the adjustment occurring in 1983–85), tight monetary policy, and active exchange rate policy to improve competitiveness; the next phase (1986–93) emphasized greater trade liberalization and deregulation, extensive tax reforms, financial market reform, and reforms of pricing policies and state enterprises. In this phase, the nominal exchange rate was anchored to a currency basket, apart from small step devaluations in 1990 and 1992.

Senegal

During the late 1970s and early 1980s, a succession of droughts, deterioration of the terms of trade, and inappropriate policies resulted in large fiscal and external current account deficits and a rising external debt. After a period of unsuccessful stabilization efforts, sustained adjustment was achieved during 1983–88 founded on substantial fiscal consolidation and structural reforms. Together with more favorable terms of trade and weather conditions this led to an improved economic performance. But the gains were not long-lasting: in 1989–93, financial policies weakened, structural reform stalled, and external competitiveness continued to deteriorate in the face of adverse terms of trade shocks. In early 1994, adjustment efforts were renewed and the CFA franc was devalued by 50 percent.

Thailand

The expansionary public sector policies of the late 1970s resulted in growing fiscal and external imbalances and left the Thai economy in a vulnerable position when it faced the external shocks of 1980–82. Following a brief period when adjustment measures produced only marginal improvements, a major adjustment effort was undertaken in 1984–85, when the baht was devalued, significant fiscal consolidation began, and a decisive change was made in the orientation of trade and industrial policies toward export-led growth. Since 1987, Thailand has been in the midst of an investment- and export-led economic boom with large accompanying capital inflows.

be a protracted and continuous process and is by no means complete in many of the countries considered. The periods were chosen to correspond as closely as possible to a phase during which a distinct approach to macroeconomic and structural adjustment was being pursued (Table 1; see Box 1 for summaries of the policy strategy pursued in each case). The choice of periods does not necessarily correspond precisely to the timing of IMF-supported programs; in many cases there had been earlier programs that were either quickly interrupted or were followed by a re-emergence of external imbalances at a later stage (Chart 1). Moreover, some important policy changes took place within the identified periods (for example, the shift to exchange-rate-based stabilization in Chile in 1978); consequently, the discussion in some sections of the study will focus on different time periods.

Long-Term Trends in Growth and Investment

Before discussing the response to adjustment policies, it is instructive to examine the long-term growth record in the eight countries (Charts 2 and 3). A comparison of broad period averages of growth rates across countries and over time, and the use of

Table 1. Adjustment Periods in the Eight Countries

	Period I	Period II
Bangladesh[1]	1980/81–1984/85	1985/86–1993/94
Chile	1974–82	1983–89
Ghana	1983–86	1987–91
India[2]	1991/92–1992/93	...
Mexico	1983–87	1988–93
Morocco	1981–85	1986–93
Senegal	1984–88	1989–93
Thailand	1981–86	1987–93

[1]Fiscal year runs from July to June.
[2]Fiscal year runs from April to March.

residual, typically referred to as growth in total factor productivity (TFP), suggest a number of observations (Table 2).[10] First, the wide variations in

simple growth accounting exercises that decompose real GDP growth into the relative contributions from physical and human capital accumulation and a

[10]Disentangling the underlying growth in potential output from cyclical developments and supply shocks is always difficult and can be especially complicated in the case of severe recessions (Chile, 1975 and 1982) or where supply shocks are large and frequent (Morocco and Senegal). TFP measures can also be a misleading indicator of underlying productivity developments if major structural changes make part of the capital stock obsolete. The growth accounting exercises involve imposing a common production function on all of the countries as well as a series of assumptions concerning the initial level of the capital stock and rate of depreciation; see the footnotes to Table 2 for details. The estimates for TFP in Chile, Mexico, and Thailand are broadly comparable to those reported in Bosworth and others (1994), Elías (1992), and Tinakorn and Sussangkarn (1994), respectively. A set of alternative estimates was also prepared using a production function that includes human capital, following an approach similar to Mankiw, Romer, and Weil (1992), but allowing for differences in efficiency because of changes in the age profile of the population. Both of the estimated TFP measures tend to overestimate cyclical movements in productivity (for example, because of lack of data on changes in man-hours worked).

Chart 1. IMF Arrangements in the Eight Countries[1]

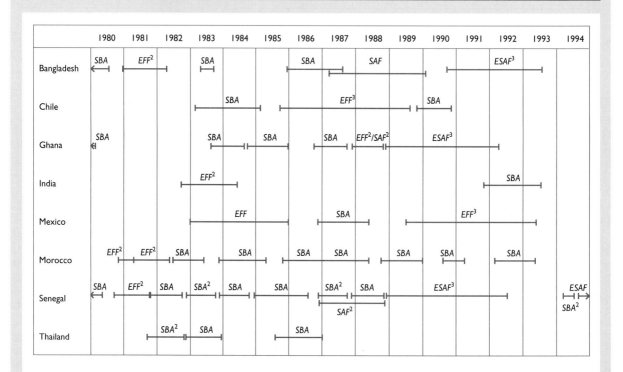

[1]EFF = extended Fund facility; ESAF = enhanced structural adjustment facility; SAF = structural adjustment facility; and SBA = stand-by arrangement.
[2]Arrangement canceled prior to initial expiration date.
[3]Arrangement extended beyond initial expiration date.

Chart 2. Real Per Capita GDP Growth, 1970–94
(Period averages; in percent)

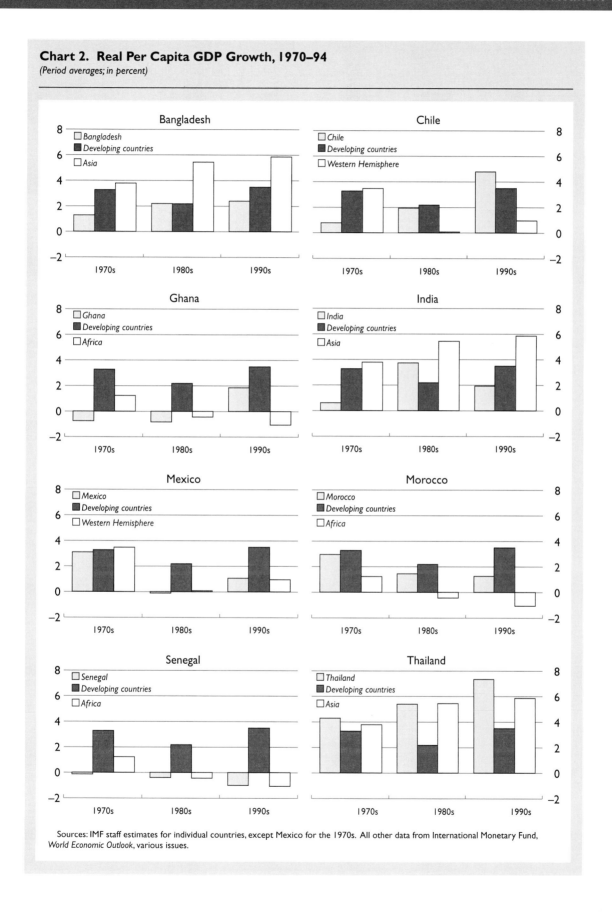

Sources: IMF staff estimates for individual countries, except Mexico for the 1970s. All other data from International Monetary Fund, *World Economic Outlook*, various issues.

Chart 3.   Real Per Capita GDP Growth and Investment Ratios
(In percent)

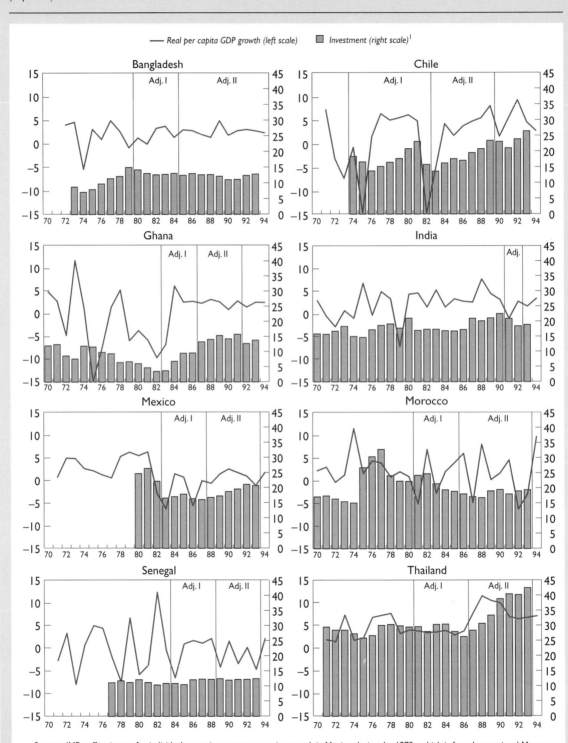

Sources: IMF staff estimates for individual countries, except per capita growth in Mexico during the 1970s, which is from International Monetary Fund, *World Economic Outlook*, various issues.

[1]Total fixed investment (public and private) at constant prices as a ratio to GDP, except for Ghana which is at current prices.

Table 2. Factors Influencing Growth, 1970–93

(Annual averages in percent, unless otherwise indicated)

	Bangladesh		Chile		Ghana		India		Mexico		Morocco[1]		Senegal		Thailand	
	1970–82	1983–93	1970–82	1983–93	1970–82	1983–93	1970–82	1983–93	1970–82	1983–93	1970–82	1983–94	1970–82	1983–93	1970–82	1983–93
Investment/GDP[2]	10.6	12.4	16.8	22.6	8.9	11.8	20.6	21.3	25.9	18.1	23.2	19.8	11.0	11.8	31.1	34.5
Savings/GDP[3]	2.9	7.1	9.4	17.0	8.3	10.2	19.5	20.7	18.0	20.1	16.4	21.2	9.9	6.3	22.7	29.3
Real GDP growth[4]	1.0	4.6	1.1	5.7	—	4.3	3.4	5.2	6.2	1.4	5.1	3.7	2.8	1.8	6.7	8.3
Contributions to growth from																
Capital	0.3	1.2	1.1	1.3	0.6	0.5	1.5	2.0	2.9	1.3	3.0	1.6	0.9	1.0	4.0	3.6
Labor	1.5	1.8	1.5	1.2	1.4	1.8	1.5	1.4	2.1	1.9	2.0	1.9	1.4	1.5	2.2	1.7
Total factor productivity (TFP)[5]	-0.8	1.6	-1.5	3.2	-2.1	1.9	0.4	1.8	1.2	-1.8	0.1	0.2	0.5	-0.8	0.4	3.0
Change in capital-labor ratio	-1.8	0.1	0.1	0.8	-0.8	-1.7	1.1	2.3	3.6	—	4.0	0.8	-0.1	0.8	6.0	5.3
Alternative measure of TFP growth[6]	-0.4	2.1	-1.0	3.4	-2.9	2.1	0.1	1.8	1.7	-1.7	-0.4	—	-1.4	-1.7	1.4	3.6
	1970	1990	1970	1990	1970	1990	1970	1990	1970	1990	1970	1990	1970	1990	1970	1990
Indicators of human capital accumulation																
Effective labor supply[7]	0.93	0.92	1.07	1.22	0.89	0.89	1.04	1.11	0.87	1.06	0.88	1.00	0.92	0.90	0.89	1.18
Primary school enrollment ratio (percent)[8]	54	77	107	98	64	77	73	98	104	115	52	65	41	59	83	90
Mean years of primary education	2.0	2.4	5.1	6.1	2.1	3.6	1.5	2.5	3.6	4.9	0.9	1.9	0.6	1.7	4.0	5.0

Sources: IMF staff estimates; International Monetary Fund, *World Economic Outlook*, various issues; World Bank, *World Tables*; World Bank, *Social Indicators*; Barro and Lee (1993); Nehru and Dhareshwar (1993); and Sarel (1995).

[1]Averages for Morocco include an estimate for 1994, owing to a large drought-related decline in GDP and investment in 1992 and 1993.

[2]Measured in constant prices, except Mexico, Chile during the first subperiod, and Ghana, which are in current prices. Due to lack of data, average for first subperiod for Bangladesh starts in 1973, Chile in 1974, Senegal in 1977, and Mexico in 1980. Bangladesh is gross fixed investment only.

[3]Gross national savings.

[4]GDP growth and the contributions are compound annual averages. Contributions to growth are calculated with a Cobb-Douglas production function; assigning weights of 0.4 and 0.6 to capital and labor, respectively. Contributions may not add to total growth because of rounding.

[5]TFP residuals should be interpreted with some care, since they include cyclical fluctuations in factor utilization and can therefore be sensitive to the choice of subperiods. This is especially noticeable for Chile. They are also sensitive to the measurement of factor inputs, which may be a particular problem during periods of rapid structural reform. For example, measurement errors may account for the negative TFP growth estimated for Mexico during the 1980s.

[6]Derived after taking account of changes in quality because of changes in age-efficiency of the labor force and education. Calculated with a Cobb-Douglas production function assigning weights of one third to capital, one third to labor, and one third to human capital. See Mankiw, Romer, and Weil (1992).

[7]The effective labor supply is a relative measure, taken from Sarel (1995), which reflects the age structure of the population and the estimated productivity of different age groups. An effective labor supply equal to unity corresponds to the average demographic distribution in a sample of 119 countries; a higher number indicates that the population is more concentrated around high-productivity age groups.

[8]Gross enrollment ratios, that is, the total number of enrollees in primary school relative to the total population at primary school age. This ratio may exceed 100 when children outside the primary school age group are enrolled in primary school.

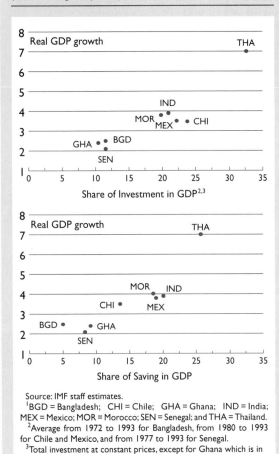

Chart 4. GDP Growth, Investment, and National Saving, 1970–93[1]
(Annual averages; in percent)

Source: IMF staff estimates.
[1]BGD = Bangladesh; CHI = Chile; GHA = Ghana; IND = India; MEX = Mexico; MOR = Morocco; SEN = Senegal; and THA = Thailand.
[2]Average from 1972 to 1993 for Bangladesh, from 1980 to 1993 for Chile and Mexico, and from 1977 to 1993 for Senegal.
[3]Total investment at constant prices, except for Ghana which is in current prices. Gross fixed investment for Bangladesh.

investment and saving rates across the countries appear to account for an important part of the differences in growth rates. For example, capital deepening in Thailand has been considerable, because of high investment supported by high saving rates. At the other extreme, average investment and saving rates in Bangladesh, Ghana, and Senegal have been low (Chart 4). However, there have also been marked changes in particular countries' investment and saving performance over time, and these will be discussed further below.

Second, although human capital accumulation is difficult to measure accurately, indicators based on levels of education suggest that Bangladesh, Ghana, India, Morocco, and Senegal began with markedly lower human capital stocks, measured by the coverage of primary education. Third, changes in the age profile of the population can have important effects

on growth since productivity is likely to vary with age.[11] As discussed later, these demographic factors also appear to have had a substantial influence on saving rates. Over the last several decades, the demographic profiles least favorable to growth have been those of Bangladesh, Ghana, India, and Senegal (reflecting the large proportion of young in the population), whereas the age profile in Thailand has been especially favorable to growth.

The estimates of TFP growth are, by their nature, residuals; consequently, they may be subject to considerable margins of error especially during periods of substantial structural reform when output may be underestimated (because of changes in the production structure that are not adequately captured by national income accounts statistics) and net investment overestimated (because of large relative price shifts that render part of the existing capital stock economically obsolescent). For example, both factors were probably important in the case of Mexico, although the lack of data does not allow them to be taken into account in the empirical estimates.[12]

Initial Conditions

The economic structure of the eight countries was quite diverse (Table 3). Agriculture accounted for over one third of GDP in three of the countries (Bangladesh, Ghana, and India) in 1980; these countries also had relatively closed economies, with the ratio of imports and of exports to GDP typically less than 10 percent. By contrast, in the other five countries (Chile, Mexico, Morocco, Senegal, and Thailand) industry produced a larger share of GDP (some 30 percent or more) than agriculture, and they had more open economies. For a number of the countries (India, Thailand, and, increasingly, Chile and Mexico, were the exceptions) exports tended to be concentrated in a few primary commodities.

The magnitude of macroeconomic imbalances at the start of adjustment was greatly influenced by the size and nature of exogenous shocks in preceding years and by the initial policy responses to them (Table 4 and Chart 5).[13] Over half of the countries

---

[11]Sarel (1995) estimates an age-related productivity structure which suggests that, on average, workers reach peak productivity between their thirties and fifties.

[12]In Mexico, the current methodology for estimating the national accounts, which has not been updated since 1980, is also thought to introduce a downward bias in GDP growth since oil has an excessive weight in total output.

[13]Because conditions prior to the two adjustment periods in Chile were so different, they are discussed separately. Chile I refers to the adjustment period that began in 1974 following the advent of the Pinochet regime and Chile II refers to the stabilization period following the collapse of the exchange-rate-based stabilization strategy in 1982.

Table 3. Economic Structure in 1980

	GDP Per Capita (1987 US$)	Structure of Production (In percent of GDP)		Merchandise Trade (In percent of GDP)		Major Export[1] (In percent of merchandise trade)	Broad Money (In percent of GDP)
		Agriculture	Industry	Exports	Imports		
Mexico	1,927	9	35	8	10	Oil (62)	29
Chile	1,586	8	42	17	20	Copper (45)	26
Morocco	781	18	31	13	20	Phosphate (42)	42
Thailand	718	26	32	20	26	Rice (17)[2]	23
Senegal	668	27[3]	27[3]	18	33	Groundnuts (39)[3]	28
Ghana	435	60	12	7	6	Cocoa (72)	19
India	262	38	26	5[4]	9[4]	Manufactures (67)	39
Bangladesh	142	52	17	5[4]	18[4]	Jute (69)[4]	16

Sources: World Bank, *World Tables;* International Monetary Fund, *International Financial Statistics;* and IMF staff estimates.

[1] Includes derivatives or closely related products of the commodity.

[2] 1981; manufactures account for 30 percent of merchandise exports.

[3] 1979.

[4] 1980/81.

Table 4. Initial Macroeconomic Imbalances and Structural Distortions

Country	Severe External Financing Constraint During Initial Adjustment?	Followed by Rescheduling of Debt?	Initial Fiscal Imbalance	High Inflation	Size of Initial External Imbalances	Adverse External Shocks	Extent of Structural Distortions
			(In preadjustment period)				
Most severe initial macroeconomic problems							
Chile I	No	No	Large	Yes	Small	Large	Intermediate
Chile II	Yes	Yes	Small[1]	No	Large	Large	Small
Ghana	Partial[2]	No	Intermediate	Yes	Small[2]	Intermediate	Large
India	Yes	No	Intermediate	No	Intermediate	Intermediate	Large
Mexico	Yes	Yes	Large	Yes	Large	Small	Intermediate
Morocco	Yes	Yes	Large	No	Large	Large	Intermediate
Senegal	Yes	Yes	Intermediate	No	Large	Intermediate	Large
Other countries							
Bangladesh	No	No	Intermediate	No	Intermediate	Small	Large
Thailand	No	No	Small	No	Intermediate	Large	Small

Note: Preadjustment period refers to the four-year period preceding the start of the first adjustment period. For Chile II the preadjustment period is 1979–82. Size of initial external imbalance refers to the external debt-GDP ratio and the current account deficit (as percent of GDP) in the preadjustment period. "Large" indicates that the debt ratio was 40 percent or higher and the current account deficit ratio was 5 percent or higher. "Intermediate" indicates that the debt ratio was between 20 percent and 40 percent and/or the current account deficit ratio was between 3 percent and 5 percent. "Small" indicates that these ratios were below 20 percent and 3 percent, respectively. Adverse external shock refers to the aggregate size of shocks related to the terms of trade, changes in interest rates on external debt, and global demand (see McCarthy, Neary, and Zanalda (1994)). "Large" is defined as a cumulative shock during the four-year period with an impact effect of more than 4 percent of GDP. "Intermediate" is a cumulative shock between 2 percent and 4 percent, and "small" is a shock of less than 2 percent. Fiscal imbalance refers to the ratio of the average central government fiscal deficit to GDP during the period. "Large" indicates a deficit of 10 percent or higher, "moderate" indicates a deficit between 5 percent and 10 percent, and "small" a deficit below 5 percent. High inflation indicates whether average annual consumer price index inflation was at least 20 percent during the period. Structural distortions refer to the extent of structural distortions in the 1970s as discussed in Section VIII.

[1] Does not include central bank quasi-fiscal deficits.

[2] Prior to the Economic Recovery Program in 1983, Ghana's access to external financing was severely curtailed and extensive foreign exchange rationing was in place. However, official external financing increased substantially once the program was adopted.

Chart 5. Indicators of Domestic and External Economic Performance During Preadjustment Period and During 1990–93

(In percent, unless otherwise specified)

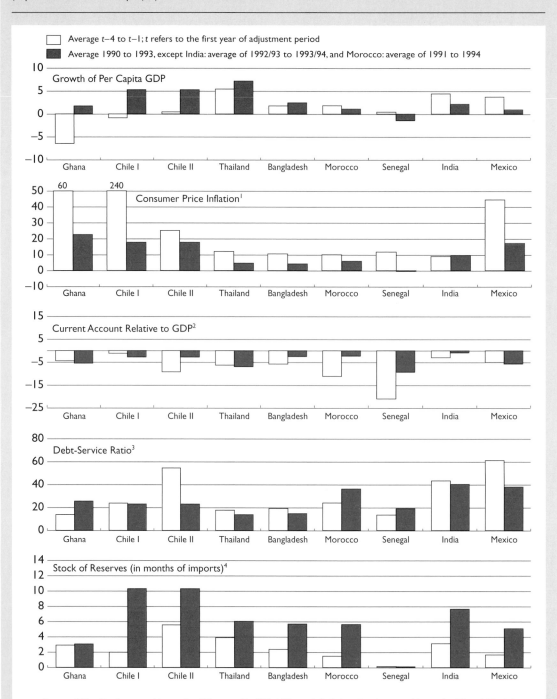

Sources: IMF staff estimates; and International Monetary Fund, *World Economic Outlook*, various issues, and *International Financial Statistics*.
[1] Average of CPI inflation rates at end of period whenever possible. For Bangladesh, Ghana, and Morocco, average of annual averages.
[2] Current account balance excludes official grants.
[3] Scheduled debt service (after rescheduling, if applicable) in percent of exports of goods and services; merchandise exports for India and Thailand; goods and services plus private transfers for Bangladesh and Morocco. For Morocco and Mexico, the first average is $t-3$ to $t-1$, and for Bangladesh, it is $t-1$ only, due to the lack of data.
[4] Gross reserves. For Bangladesh, the first average is $t-2$ to $t-1$.

(especially Chile I, Morocco, Senegal, and Thailand) were subjected to large adverse external shocks in the preadjustment period, resulting primarily from a combination of higher oil prices, declining commodity export prices, and rising world interest rates (Chart 6). The nature of the crisis and the severity of the associated external financing constraints were typically heavily influenced by the initial policy response to the macroeconomic problems that resulted from these shocks. In most cases, expansionary policies, mainly in the form of large fiscal deficits, had contributed to higher inflation or rising external debt burdens or both that eventually proved unmanageable (Chile I, Ghana, India, Mexico, Morocco, and Senegal). External financing constraints were manifested early in the process in Chile I (1970–73) and in Ghana (before 1983), and the initial policy response was a massive intensification of import and exchange controls. Consequently, demand pressures in these cases were largely reflected in very high inflation rather than increased foreign borrowing. By contrast, in Chile II, the initial macroeconomic imbalance reflected a massive boom in private sector demand fueled by a surge in private credit and heavy external borrowing.

Most of the countries suffered from extensive structural distortions, stemming from excessive government intervention in the economy. Distortions were the most severe in Bangladesh, Ghana, India, and Senegal, which had a history of inward-oriented development policies, relying on high and complex trade barriers, official price controls, and large public sectors. Only Thailand and Chile II had relatively small distortions when they began their adjustment efforts.

Most of the countries began adjustment with their external positions under pressure, in the form of low reserves, accumulating arrears, or debt-service burdens that implied a large net transfer of resources abroad (the latter most notably in the case of the market borrowers that lost access to international financial markets—Chile, Morocco, and, especially, Mexico). By the early 1990s, however, these positions had improved in most cases. First, official reserves rose considerably, to well above the equivalent of three months of imports except in Ghana and Senegal.[14] Second, by 1993 only Senegal was accumulating external arrears—in all other countries there was no outstanding stock of arrears. Third, in half of the countries, current account positions had improved—typically with the largest improvements in those cases where initial imbalances were largest (see Chart 5). In countries that registered a widening

of current account deficits, this was accompanied in most cases by a sizable increase in capital inflows. At the same time, scheduled debt-service ratios (after taking account of debt and debt-service restructuring) fell in over half of the countries, most notably in Chile and Mexico.

The Response of Growth to Adjustment

At the risk of some oversimplification, and anticipating some of the results discussed in Sections III–IX, the growth response following the adoption of adjustment policies in the eight countries can be summarized as follows. In considering these overall developments, the intrinsic difficulties of drawing strong conclusions about the effects of policies on growth and distinguishing these effects from other influences, including changes in the external environment and other exogenous shocks, should be recognized.

Responses in the Short Term

• In several countries (most notably Chile in both 1975 and 1982 and Mexico in 1982–83) output and investment rates initially declined severely, reflecting in part the reversal of previous investment booms, as well as a sharp deterioration in measured productivity that was probably due in large part to a decline in capacity utilization. Employment data is sketchy for many countries, but unemployment was especially severe in Chile, reaching an unprecedented 20 percent in 1982. Where inflation was high (Chile, Mexico, and Ghana), it generally appears to have exacerbated the poor initial growth performance. Although it is difficult to identify the direction of causation, this accords with evidence from broader cross-country studies, which suggest that episodes of macroeconomic instability, including high inflation, are typically associated with lower growth.

• Most other countries (India, Morocco, Senegal, and Thailand) experienced more moderate initial slowdowns in growth, while no discernible slowdown took place in Bangladesh. Private investment as a share of GDP typically fell for several years, while cuts in public investment were part of the fiscal consolidation in most cases (Table 5 and Chart 7). However, the investment decline in Thailand was relatively shallow and short-lived.

• Following a prolonged period of economic decline and severe import compression, growth in Ghana picked up quickly, once the Economic Recovery Program was implemented in 1983, reflecting a marked turnaround in productivity and a mod-

---

[14]Senegal has access to the common pool of reserves shared by all the members of the CFA franc zone.

Chart 6. Size of External Shocks[1]
(In percent of GDP)

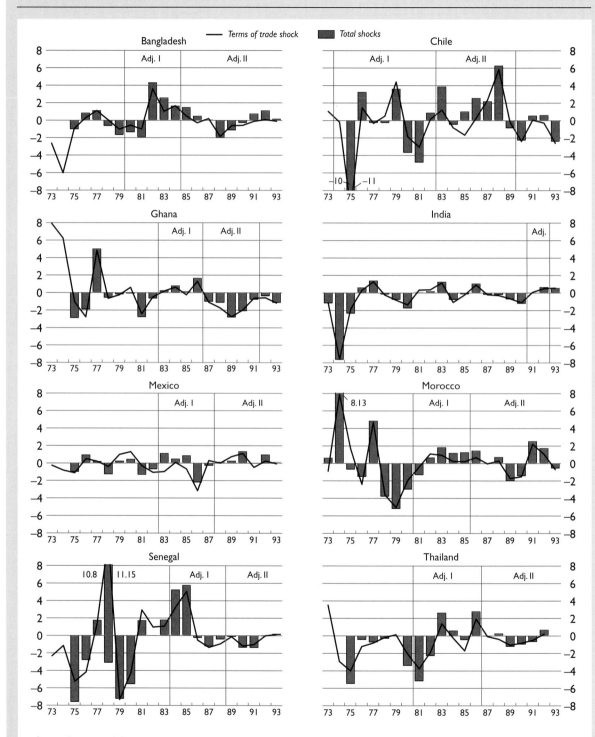

Sources: International Monetary Fund, *World Economic Outlook,* various issues; and IMF staff estimates.
[1]The total shock indicates the combined impact effect, in percent of GDP, of changes in the trade-weighted terms of trade, fluctuations in world interest rates affecting debt-service payments, and changes in global demand. A positive number implies a favorable shock. See McCarthy, Neary, and Zanalda (1994).

Table 5. Response of Private Investment During Adjustment Periods

(Percentage changes in GDP over the indicated period; in constant prices, unless otherwise indicated)

Country	Investment Decline from Peak to Trough (In percent of GDP)	Duration of Investment "Pause" Between Decline and Start of Recovery	Magnitude of Investment Takeoff (In percent of GDP)
		Corresponding period	
Bangladesh	2.8 (1980–90)	Prolonged stagnation	Weak recovery (1990–93)
Chile[1]	9.3 (1981–83)	No pause (steep decline followed by sustained recovery)	12.0 (1983–93)
Ghana[2]	3.1 (1985–86)	No pause, but early recovery after 1983 interrupted by a decline in 1986	Weak, uneven recovery
India[3]	3.1 (1990/91–1992/93)	At least 2 years	Recovery appears to have begun in 1994/95
Mexico	4.4 (1981–83)	About 4 years (1983–87)	5.5 (1987–93)
Morocco	2.9 (1982–85)	About 3 years (1985–88)	Weak, uneven recovery (1989–93)
Senegal[1]	No significant decline	No pause	No significant recovery
Thailand	3.4 (1983–86)	About 1 year (1986)	14.8 (1986–93)

Source: IMF staff estimates.

[1]Nongovernment investment.

[2]Current prices.

[3]Excludes inventories and that part of statistical discrepancy attributed to investment in the national income accounts. Including these items would show a sharper initial decline. Although full data are not yet available, a variety of evidence points to a resurgence of private investment in India during 1994/95 (see Chopra and others (1995)).

erate pickup in (mainly public) investment, financed in part by higher official external financing.

Responses in the Medium Term

• Simple time-series comparisons as well as the results of panel regressions based on a control-group approach using data for a large number of countries suggest that Thailand, Chile, and, to a lesser extent, Ghana, have sustained growth higher than that achieved prior to the adoption of adjustment policies. Although cyclical recovery was obviously part of the story, especially in Chile, the improvements in productivity have persisted for long enough to suggest that other influences, including structural reform, were also at work. Chile and, even more emphatically, Thailand were also the two countries that achieved large and sustained improvements in private investment, supported by higher domestic sav-

ing as well as capital inflows—suggesting a shift to a path where higher saving and higher growth were mutually supporting.

• In many other countries (including India, Mexico, and Morocco), the initial recovery in private investment was slower; in many cases, an investment "pause" of from two–four years occurred before private investment began to respond to improved macroeconomic balances and structural reform measures (see Table 4).

• In Mexico, the recovery in private investment, albeit delayed, was eventually quite significant. However, this recovery did not translate into substantially higher rates of recorded output growth. Moreover, the eventual resumption of capital inflows coincided with a collapse in private saving, leading to large current account deficits that eventually proved unsustainable. The limited output response occurred despite major progress in several key struc-

Chart 7. Share of Private and Public Investment in GDP

(In percent; constant prices unless otherwise indicated)

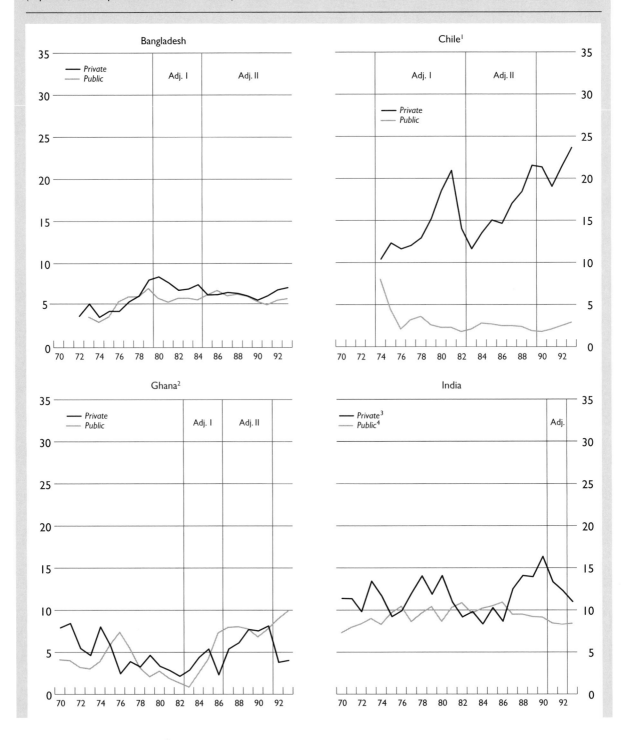

Chart 7 *(concluded)*

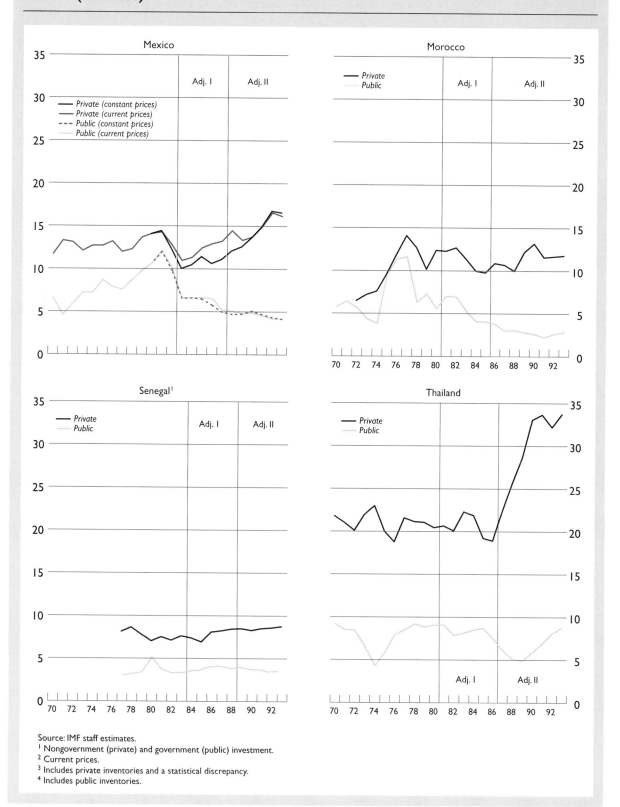

Source: IMF staff estimates.
[1] Nongovernment (private) and government (public) investment.
[2] Current prices.
[3] Includes private inventories and a statistical discrepancy.
[4] Includes public inventories.

Chart 8. Structural Reforms and Trends in Total Factor Productivity[1]

(Total factor productivity contribution to GDP growth; annual averages in percent)

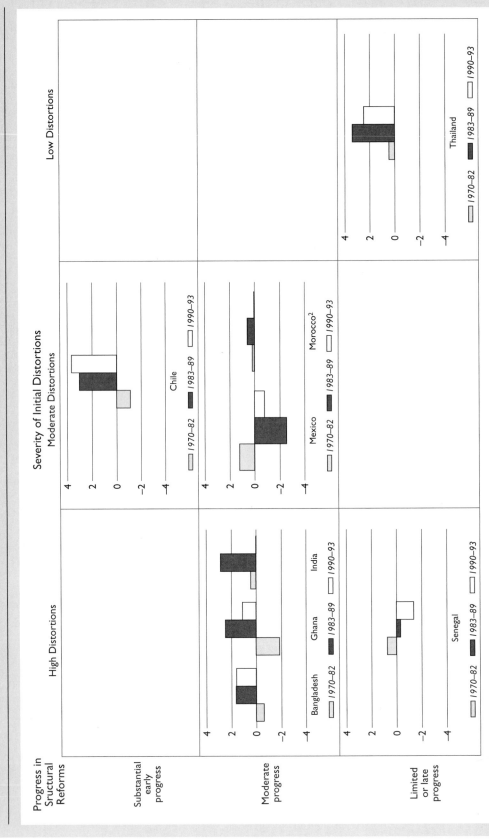

Sources: IMF staff estmates; International Monetary Fund, *World Economic Outlook*, various issues; World Bank, *World Tables*; World Bank Social Indicators database; Barro and Lee (1993); Nehru and Dhareshwar (1993); and Sarel (1995).
[1] The total factor productivity contributions should be interpreted with care, because they include cyclical changes in factor utilization.
[2] For Morocco, the third average includes the year 1994, during which the economy recovered from the effects of the severe drought of 1992–93.

tural areas and was especially striking in light of the tendency—suggested by some recent cross-country studies and reaffirmed for the other countries in the study that experienced high-inflation episodes (Chile and Ghana)—for output growth and measured productivity to recover quite strongly after inflation falls (see Section IV). Without claiming to have a complete answer, important contributory factors, in addition to the measurement problems discussed earlier, appear to have been the late or incomplete nature of structural reforms in the agricultural sector and the market for infrastructural services as well as a persistence of high margins on financial intermediation. Several measures in these areas were implemented relatively recently and have not yet had a major impact on output.[15]

• Despite no initial slowdown in investment or output growth and notwithstanding the progress that has been made toward macroeconomic stability, Bangladesh has not yet achieved a shift to a markedly higher growth path.

---

[15]There are signs that, prior to the recent crisis, the reforms were beginning to yield significant gains, most notably in the manufacturing sector, where average output per worker rose at an annual rate of 6 percent during the period 1988–94.

• The recovery in growth was weakest in Senegal, especially after the track record of macroeconomic stability is taken into account.

• It has typically been difficult—in this and other studies—to establish robust empirical evidence on the links between productivity growth and structural policies, in part because it is hard to distill complex structural policy measures into a few quantifiable variables.[16] Nevertheless, an examination of overall trends in productivity growth suggests that those countries that made the most substantial progress in removing structural distortions (Chile) or where such distortions were not severe to begin with (Thailand) generally experienced the most rapid and sustained improvements in measured TFP (Chart 8). Other countries that experienced considerable initial productivity gains were those that began with severe structural distortions and made moderate progress in removing them (notably Ghana and, to a lesser extent, Bangladesh and India). Countries that began with severe distortions and made only limited progress with structural reforms (Senegal) tended to have sluggish TFP growth.

---

[16]These issues are discussed in more depth in Section VIII.

III Cross-Country Evidence on Factors Influencing Growth

This section draws upon cross-country evidence for as large a group of countries as possible, to examine some of the long-term influences on growth and the role of several policy-related variables. With the aid of a control group and econometric estimates of the long-term determinants of growth, shifts in the growth performance of the eight countries during various adjustment periods are examined. Broad conclusions are summarized here and details of the econometric exercises are discussed in Appendix II.

Correlations Between Growth and Policy-Related Variables

Using a growth-accounting approach, output growth is decomposed into the contribution made by capital accumulation, labor force growth, and total factor productivity (TFP). The links between policies and growth and the channels through which these links operate are then examined by regressing, in turn, real GDP growth, the rate of increase of the capital stock, and the rate of TFP growth on a set of policy-related variables using panel (that is, across countries and over time) data for a large group of countries over the period 1970–92. Several broad relationships are suggested, but the limitations of the approach should be borne in mind when interpreting the results. Given the inherent difficulty of constructing simple measures of policy variables, it is necessary to use proxies that are also affected by non-policy-related factors. Moreover, the exercise identifies correlations, but does not shed any light on the direction of causality and should not be regarded as a structural equation explaining growth.

Macroeconomic instability (as measured by inflation, fiscal deficits, and parallel exchange market premiums) is significantly negatively correlated with growth. The links appear to operate through a dampening of both investment and productivity. Of course, causality is not unidirectional—for example, in the event of an adverse exogenous shock, causation could run from investment and growth to inflation and the fiscal balance. Evidence from other studies also suggests that the links between inflation

and growth are nonlinear, with high inflation much more likely to be associated with slower growth than moderate inflation.[17] In such cases, high inflation is probably acting in part as a proxy for complex effects associated with a loss of macroeconomic control and the consequent undermining of private sector confidence.

Structural distortions in the trade and financial systems, as well as low educational attainment, are also negatively correlated with output growth, with the effects operating both through productivity growth and capital accumulation. The cross-country evidence also suggests that favorable terms of trade movements are positively correlated with growth.

Based on these correlations, which policies appear to have influenced long-term growth in the eight countries? Although these variables together explain only a relatively small proportion of the variation in growth across countries and time, the correlations suggest some broad conclusions.[18]

• Over the entire period being examined, Chile, Mexico, and Ghana experienced much higher inflation rates than the other countries in the present study; Ghana and Bangladesh also had especially large exchange market distortions (see Appendix II, Table 15), suggesting that macroeconomic instability would tend to have dampened growth in these countries.

• As for structural factors, Bangladesh, Ghana, and India generally had the most restrictive trade regimes; Bangladesh and Ghana also had the least developed financial sectors. Human capital formation as measured by educational attainment was especially low in Bangladesh, Ghana, India, Morocco, and Senegal. The correlations discussed above would suggest that these structural distortions and weaknesses are likely to have hindered long-term growth in these countries.

---

[17] The results of Bruno and Easterly (1995) suggest that growth falls sharply during episodes of high (which they define as above 40 percent per annum) inflation, and generally recovers strongly after inflation is stabilized. Sarel (1996) suggests that the negative influences of inflation on growth begin to be significant at lower inflation rates (that is, above 8–10 percent per annum).

[18] The adjusted R-squared was typically in the range 0.1 to 0.3.

• In contrast, Thailand's track record of macroeconomic stability, relatively high degree of human capital formation, and relatively open trade system could be expected to be associated with higher growth, capital accumulation, and productivity gains.

Of course, substantial changes in policies took place over the course of the period of more than two decades considered here. All three of the countries that experienced episodes of very high inflation—Ghana, Chile, and Mexico—lowered inflation substantially over time, while Bangladesh and Ghana also succeeded in reducing considerably their exchange market distortions. The next section examines whether, on the basis of panel data evidence, these achievements appear to have been associated, over time, with higher growth.

Evidence on Shifts in Growth Across Adjustment Periods

Shifts over time in the growth performance of the eight countries are examined using as many other countries as possible as the control group. The approach compares the actual per capita growth performance in each of the eight economies with a counterfactual that is the "world average" growth performance after controlling for key influences—physical and human capital accumulation, technological "catching up," and terms of trade movements—common to the growth experience of all countries. Using a panel regression framework, growth differentials—which can be interpreted as measures of how each country's per capita growth differed from the world average in each period after controlling for the above factors—are calculated over each identified adjustment phase for each country.[19] A second set of growth differentials is estimated by including the quantifiable proxies for macroeconomic policies discussed above (inflation, fiscal deficits, and parallel market exchange premiums) in the regressions (Chart 9). One would gener-

ally expect the remaining growth differentials to be smaller once account is taken of these policy-related variables.[20] For example, Chart 9 shows that, after taking into account the influence of factor accumulation, technological convergence, and changes in the terms of trade, Mexico's growth shifted from rates well above the world average before the debt crisis in 1982 to rates significantly below during the five years following the crisis. When variables proxying the effects of macroeconomic policies are also controlled for, the growth differential in the crisis period is smaller and loses its statistical significance, and in the postcrisis period growth shows no strong rebound relative to the world average (0.7 percent per annum); see Appendix II, Table 17. These findings suggest, first, that periods of severe macroeconomic instability are inimical to growth, and, second, that the absence of a strong recovery in the period since 1988 is especially unusual in view of the considerable progress made in fiscal adjustment and disinflation. More generally, the results suggest the following:

• Countries experiencing episodes of severe macroeconomic instability—such as Chile in the early 1970s, Ghana prior to 1983, and Mexico after the debt crisis in 1982—typically had growth rates well below world averages even after taking account of a number of identifiable influences on growth. In these cases, the remaining growth differentials were generally lower, but still significant (Chile and Ghana) in the specifications including the macroeconomic variables. This suggests that periods of macroeconomic crisis are likely to be especially harmful to growth, but that not all of the negative influences can be captured through a few summary variables. In this context, the eventual rebound in growth in Chile and Ghana appears to be associated in part with the restoration of macroeconomic stability.[21]

---

[19] The approach follows Bruno and Easterly (1995). A more appropriate counterfactual than the world average would be the postadjustment performance of each country relative to what it would have been in the absence of adjustment; in practice, however, it was not possible to estimate such counterfactuals with available information. The choice of starting year for particular subperiods was determined by the timing of implementation of major adjustment policies and was often associated with a major adverse shock. Such factors may also have an independent effect on growth; therefore estimates of the effects of policies on growth derived on the basis of the adjustment periods may be affected by reversion-to-trend biases. These issues are likely to be of greater concern for short-run changes in growth than for changes that persist over longer periods.

[20] A positive growth differential in Chart 9 implies that growth was above the world average after controlling for various determinants of growth. Owing to data limitations on proxies for structural policies, only macroeconomic variables were examined in this part of the exercise. The change in growth differential between the two estimates cannot be interpreted as representing the overall impact of policies on growth. Policies also act through investment, which is included independently in the equation. The adjusted R-squared was generally in the range of 0.3 to 0.4.

[21] These findings are confirmed by Bruno and Easterly (1995); they show that in most countries experiencing a high-inflation crisis, growth was much lower than the world average during the period of high inflation and that this differential was worse than in the precrisis period. Furthermore, most countries that reduced inflation experienced a strong rebound in their growth differential after the crisis. Mexico stands apart for the absence of a significant catching up, although its growth rate did recover to about the "world average" (after controlling for other influences).

Chart 9. Estimated Per Capita Growth Differentials
(In percentage points)

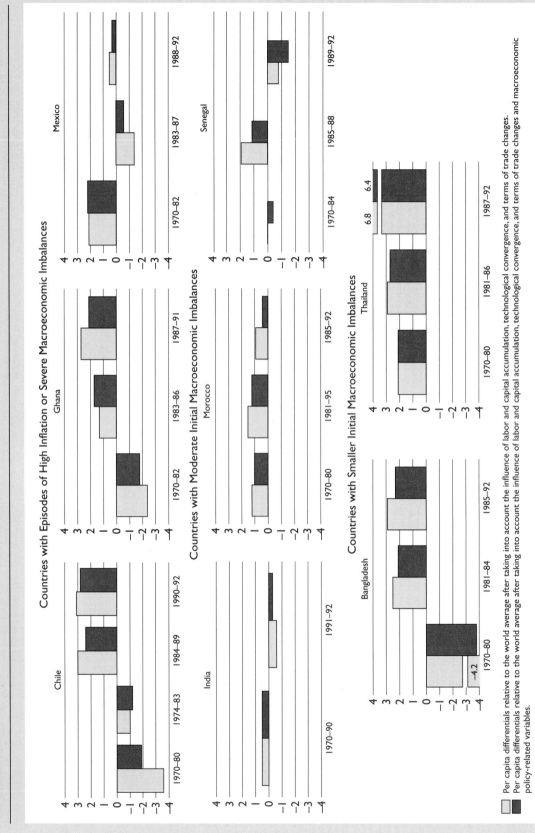

Per capita differentials relative to the world average after taking into account the influence of labor and capital accumulation, technological convergence, and terms of trade changes.

Per capita differentials relative to the world average after taking into account the influence of labor and capital accumulation, technological convergence, and terms of trade changes and macroeconomic policy-related variables.

Source: Table 16.

• The growth performance of Bangladesh during its adjustment appears more favorable once account is taken of trends in the rest of the world and factors such as its poor endowment of human capital. After controlling for such factors, its growth is above the world average. A similar judgment can be made about Morocco. Once again, the remaining growth differentials were lower after taking account of these countries' progress toward macroeconomic stability.

• In countries with long periods of macroeconomic stability, most notably Thailand, growth differentials vis-à-vis the world average are large even with the inclusion of macroeconomic policy-related variables in the equations. This suggests that many factors in addition to those incorporated in the cross-country regressions underlie the variations in growth. In addition to structural policies and broader regional influences, these may include potentially important, but hard to quantify, factors such as confidence in the government's track record on economic policy. One purpose of the case studies is to explore some of these latter influences in greater depth, while recognizing that they are often not amenable to rigorous statistical tests.

IV Role of Macroeconomic Policies

Although initial internal and external conditions varied considerably across the eight countries, in most of them the need for adjustment stemmed from an excess of domestic demand over output that had led to an unsustainable external imbalance. So the task before policymakers was to bring domestic absorption down to more sustainable levels in a way that minimized contractionary effects on output, and, at the same time, to foster conditions for raising long-term growth. This section highlights several broad themes of stabilization policies pursued by these countries, drawing where appropriate upon particular country examples, as well as the econometric analysis of private investment behavior discussed in Section V.

The output response to stabilization policies depends on a complex set of interactions among a variety of factors, including the mix of policy measures, structural features of the economy, the conditions prevailing prior to adjustment, and the impact of exogenous shocks. The three main macroeconomic policy tools used to achieve stabilization have been fiscal policy, exchange rate policy, and monetary or credit policy. These policies influence output and long-term growth through several channels: by acting on the level of aggregate demand (expenditure reduction); by influencing the ease with which demand and supply shift between the tradable and nontradable goods sectors (resource switching); and by affecting intertemporal consumption choices, that is, the composition of demand between investment and consumption.

Within this broad framework, this section centers on three main themes: how the timeliness of policy responses to emerging imbalances can greatly influence the initial impact of stabilization policies on output and investment; the importance of the consistency and sustainability of policies; and the need to take careful account of key structural rigidities in designing macroeconomic policies.

Costs of Delayed Adjustment

In most of the eight countries, adjustment had to be implemented in the context of some form of macroeconomic crisis. Thus, in all of them except Thailand and Bangladesh, the authorities were faced with uncontrolled inflation, or an abrupt deterioration in access to foreign financing, or both (see Table 3 and Chart 5). The experience of the eight countries suggests that stabilization policies undertaken because of a macroeconomic crisis will generally have more substantial, and more prolonged, contractionary effects than when policies are implemented in a more timely manner. This arises not simply because the size of initial imbalances requiring adjustment is larger, but—what is equally important—because crisis tends to spawn second-best policies and sap the private sector's confidence in government actions.

Abrupt Reduction in Real Domestic Absorption

Delays in adjustment that led to the buildup of large initial imbalances, the depletion of foreign exchange reserves, and the emergence of severe external financing constraints were often associated with a more abrupt reduction in real domestic absorption. This can be illustrated by comparing the magnitude of corrections to domestic absorption and the contemporaneous slowdown in output growth—as measured by output gaps (Table 6).[22] The largest reductions in domestic demand generally occurred in countries that had the greatest initial internal and ex-

---

[22]In the absence of reliable measures of capacity utilization for all countries, the output gap is approximated by the deviation of actual from trend real GDP. Trend GDP is estimated using a Hodrick-Prescott filter—a univariate trend extraction algorithm—on actual real GDP over the period 1970–93. The filter estimates trend GDP by minimizing the variation of actual GDP around a trend, subject to certain assumptions on the variance of the cyclical component relative to the trend component. Such measures can only be approximate and are subject to a number of potential pitfalls. For example, the estimates tend to overstate the size of output gaps in years prior to a sustained acceleration in output. Thus, the size of the output gap in Thailand in 1985–86 may be overstated. Generally, however, the estimates correspond reasonably closely with independent measures of capacity utilization for those few countries (for example, Chile, in Bosworth and others (1994)) where such measures are available.

Table 6. Changes in Domestic Absorption and Output Gaps During Particular Contractionary Episodes
(Cumulative changes in percent over indicated period; in constant prices, unless indicated otherwise)

	Initial External Current Account Balance (In percent of GDP)[1]	Change in Domestic Absorption (In percent of GDP)	Change in Estimated Output Gap (In percent of trend GDP)	Change in Real GDP	Number of Years for Output to Return to Previous Peak	Change in Primary Fiscal Balance[2]	Real Private Sector Credit Growth[3] (Annual average)
Most severe initial macroeconomic problems							
Chile I (1974–76)	–3	–14	–13	–10	4	8	55
Chile II (1981–83)	–14	–20	–24	–16	6	–4	16
Ghana (1980–82)	—	–8	–13	–10	6	3	–10
India (1990/91–1992/93)	–3	–7	–4	9	—	2	–1
Mexico (1981–83)	–7	–13	–11	–5	4	12	–3
Morocco (1981–83)	–10	–8	1	9(7)[4]	—	3	8
Other countries							
Bangladesh (1979/80–1981/82)	–6	–4	–1	5	—	1	14
Thailand (1984–86)	–5	–8	–6	10	—	—	9

Note: Senegal was not included in this part of the exercise because supply shocks were so frequent that it was not possible to estimate meaningful output gaps.

[1] Excluding transfers.

[2] Excluding grants. Positive change indicates a decrease in the deficit or an increase in the surplus.

[3] Based on the contemporaneous rate of inflation of the GDP deflator. For Bangladesh, Morocco, and Senegal, includes credit to public enterprises.

[4] The change in nonagricultural GDP is given in parentheses, to exclude the impact of weather-related supply shocks.

ternal imbalances (notably Chile and Mexico) or where existing macroeconomic problems made economies especially vulnerable to adverse external shocks. The latter were particularly large in several cases—for example, Chile I and Ghana prior to the Economic Recovery Program, as well as in Thailand (see Chart 6). For most of the countries with severe initial macroeconomic imbalances, there were few realistic alternatives to rapid and substantial stabilization; such cases were usually associated with the largest widening of output gaps and the most prolonged subsequent recessions—unless, as in Morocco, favorable supply shocks intervened.

But initial conditions and policy delays are not the only reasons for contraction. Even countries that are generally regarded as having acted in a timely manner, such as Thailand, did not escape fully from contractionary influences: although not weak by international standards, per capita growth slowed to the lowest rate in a decade during 1985–86, and the lag in the response of output and investment to adjustment policies was of concern to the authorities at the time.

Second-Best Crisis Measures

Policies undertaken in crisis conditions sometimes included ad hoc or emergency measures that were not necessarily conducive to investment and growth. Fiscal adjustment tended to be greatest in cases where the initial imbalances were largest—particularly Chile I, Mexico, and Morocco, and where loss of access to external financing forced an especially abrupt adjustment (Chart 10).[23] It is difficult to establish precise links between particular fiscal consolidation measures and growth. The reduction in public investment in these countries reversed previous booms and may well have eliminated many projects with low rates of return. However, the discussion in the companion study on the composition of fiscal

adjustment does illustrate that fiscal adjustment in such circumstances was usually not based, at least initially, on well-designed changes in tax and expenditure systems of the type thought to be conducive to growth:

> Often there is a sequencing problem, where deficiencies in public expenditure management and tax administration initially require a rather crude approach to expenditure restraint and prevent the speedy reform of the tax system. Some expenditure cuts can, however, be damaging, if not reversed in due course. To facilitate their reversal and to improve expenditure allocation, immediate action to reform both tax administration and public expenditure management is necessary.[24]

Moreover, in a number of cases (Ghana, Morocco, Mexico, and India), initial efforts to protect the balance of payments involved the imposition or intensification of import and exchange controls, which squeezed imports of intermediate and capital goods and probably added an adverse supply shock to the contractionary effects stemming from the demand side. Also, in a few countries (for example, Mexico and in Ghana on several occasions prior to the Economic Recovery Program), measures of a confiscatory nature, such as mandatory conversion of foreign currency bank deposits on nonmarket terms, further eroded private confidence.

Uncertainty and the Effectiveness of Policies

The uncertainty and loss of credibility associated with a crisis can influence the effectiveness of particular policy measures. A deterioration in private confidence, indicated by an acceleration of capital flight, is likely to have adverse consequences for growth. Beyond this, the response of the economy to policy measures may differ in several important ways, and be harder to predict, during episodes of macroeconomic crisis. These factors help to explain why a good track record of macroeconomic policies appears to make adjustment less costly.

Lower fiscal deficits affect the composition of demand by lowering the cost and increasing the availability of credit to the private sector. But these "crowding-in" effects, which would tend to offset the direct contractionary effects of fiscal consolidation, are likely to be weaker and slower to operate in conditions of economic uncertainty. In such circumstances, the rational response of private investors would be to increase the wedge they require between the cost of capital and their expected rate of return.[25] As a result, the effects of interest rate and credit poli-

---

[23] Two indicators, albeit imperfect, that can be used to examine the direct impact of fiscal policy on aggregate demand are changes in the primary fiscal balance and a fiscal impulse measure. The primary balance avoids attributing demand effects to interest payments on the large stock of external debt. The fiscal impulse measure attempts to distinguish the cyclical and discretionary components of fiscal adjustment, but "cyclical" revenue influences are likely to also reflect supply and terms of trade shocks, particularly in Ghana, Morocco, Senegal, and Mexico (the discovery of oil reserves). In practice, for the period under review, the two measures generally reveal similar patterns. Neither measure captures the potential expansionary effects that may result from expectations of lower public debt burdens in the future.

The fiscal data throughout this study relate to the consolidated central government in all countries except for Mexico (nonfinancial public sector) and Thailand (budgetary central government). For India, the central government accounts are net of tax revenues collected on behalf of the states.

[24] See Mackenzie and others (forthcoming), Section I.
[25] See the discussion in Box 3 in Section V.

Chart 10. Fiscal Indicators[1]
(In percent of GDP)

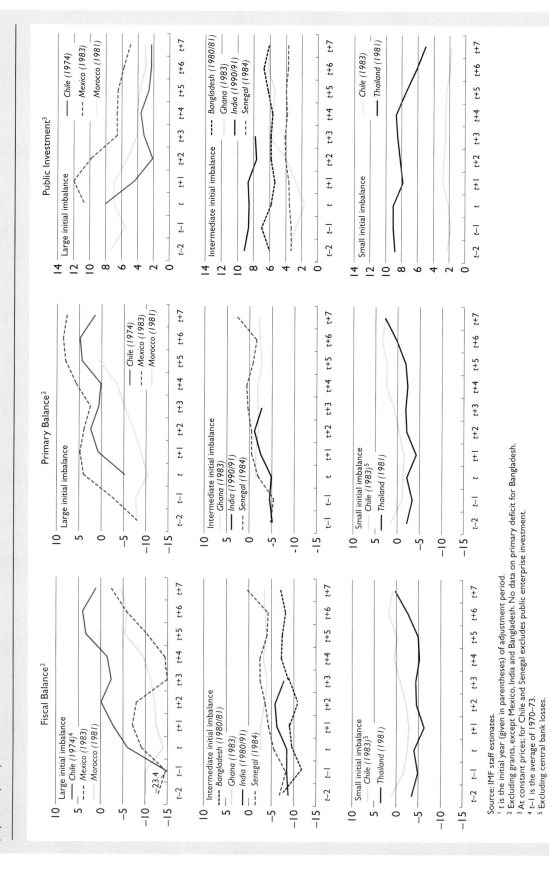

Source: IMF staff estimates.
[1] t is the initial year (given in parentheses) of adjustment period.
[2] Excluding grants, except Mexico, India and Bangladesh. No data on primary deficit for Bangladesh.
[3] At constant prices; for Chile and Senegal excludes public enterprise investment.
[4] t–1 is the average of 1970–73.
[5] Excluding central bank losses.

Chart 11. Nominal and Real Effective Exchange Rates and Inflation in Various Indexation Regimes[1]

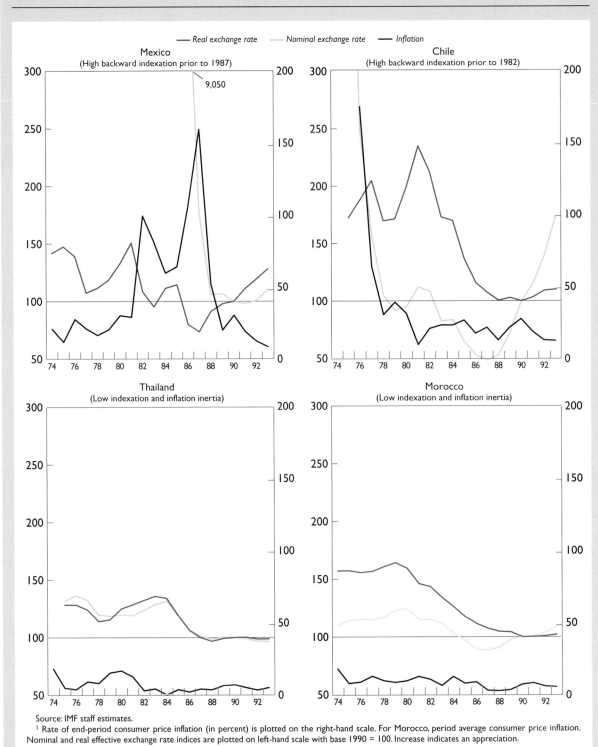

Real exchange rate   Nominal exchange rate   Inflation

Mexico
(High backward indexation prior to 1987)

9,050

Chile
(High backward indexation prior to 1982)

Thailand
(Low indexation and inflation inertia)

Morocco
(Low indexation and inflation inertia)

Source: IMF staff estimates.
[1] Rate of end-period consumer price inflation (in percent) is plotted on the right-hand scale. For Morocco, period average consumer price inflation. Nominal and real effective exchange rate indices are plotted on left-hand scale with base 1990 = 100. Increase indicates an appreciation.

cies on private sector behavior may be especially difficult to predict in the short term. In cases where adjustment was undertaken in the context of a crisis (Chile, Ghana, and Mexico), it appears that typically it took several years for credibility to be established even when substantial fiscal adjustment was undertaken up front, which contributed to the generally longer duration of the output gap. The empirical importance of such influences is hard to test, but some partial evidence is discussed in the next section.

Macroeconomic instability and heavy-handed use of government regulations prior to, and during periods of crisis, can trigger the emergence of institutional arrangements that will influence the impact of particular policy measures. For example, in countries in which a legacy of high inflation had led to widespread wage indexation (for example, Chile in the 1970s), the impact of nominal devaluations on the real exchange rate was typically greatly diminished. By contrast, a tradition of low inflation in some other countries (for example, Morocco and Thailand) allowed a more effective use of nominal depreciations to facilitate necessary changes in the real exchange rate (Chart 11).[26] Similarly, attempts to reduce inflation through a tightening of monetary policy are likely to have a more substantial contractionary effect when inflation inertia is high (for example, Chile during the money-based stabilization of 1974–75).

Less Time for Resource-Switching Policies to Take Hold

If aggregate demand declines rapidly, there is generally less time for resource-switching policies to operate sufficiently on supply, particularly of tradables, so as to minimize the contractionary effects on output. Although it is difficult to observe directly the extent of resource switching from the nontradable to the tradable goods sectors, developments in exports and imports provide some indirect indications. In most cases, the export response, although strong, typically occurred with a lag and was not sufficient to offset the initial contractionary impact on output of reductions in domestic absorption (Chart 12). Indicators of the extent and timing of resource switching in the eight countries—the strength of export and import volume growth and estimates of deviations from historical trends of the import intensity of GDP and of export market share—suggest, first, that ex-

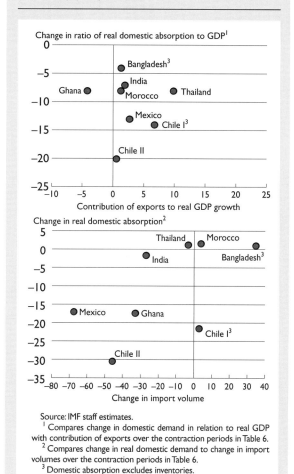

Chart 12. Changes in Domestic Absorption, Exports, and Imports During Periods of Demand Contraction
(In percentage points)

Source: IMF staff estimates.
[1] Compares change in domestic demand in relation to real GDP with contribution of exports over the contraction periods in Table 6.
[2] Compares change in real domestic demand to change in import volumes over the contraction periods in Table 6.
[3] Domestic absorption excludes inventories.

---

[26]In Ghana, under the Economic Recovery Program, inflation was reduced at the same time as the official exchange rate was massively depreciated. This depreciation did not have a large inflationary impact because the bulk of transactions were already taking place at the parallel market rate and because the nature of the economy, with its relatively small formal sector, meant that real wage rigidity was less of a factor.

port performance strengthened during the adjustment episodes in all countries except Senegal, but typically with a lag, so that it did not cushion the initial contractionary impact on output of reductions in domestic absorption. Second, beyond the initial period of demand squeeze, substantial increases in export volumes supported the strongest recoveries in output and investment in Chile (1985 onward), Ghana (1984 onward), and Thailand (1986 onward). Third, the intensification of import restrictions, which fell heavily on intermediate inputs, caused growth to suffer—in Ghana (1976–82), India (1991), and Mexico (1982). The longer-term export response is discussed in Section VIII, in the context of trade reform.

Sustainability and Consistency of Policies

Expectations of policy reversal may induce private investors to wait for uncertainty to be resolved, potentially locking the economy into a low-investment, low-growth equilibrium. In this context, the individual country studies suggest that two aspects of policies are likely to be especially important: progress toward a sustainable fiscal position and the consistency of macroeconomic policies.

Sustainability of Fiscal Policies

The effects of fiscal adjustment on output, investment, and saving depend on the composition of expenditure and revenue measures and the mix of financing, which in turn influences the pattern of real interest rates and private sector access to credit. However, expectations about the future course of fiscal policy are critical to the transmission process. If private agents expect the fiscal adjustment program to succeed in reducing the deficit and therefore the need for inflationary or debt financing, crowding-in effects will help to offset the initial contractionary effects and set in motion a virtuous circle of investment and growth.

Did private sector concerns about the medium-term sustainability of fiscal policy dampen the investment response during adjustment? There is no unique standard of fiscal sustainability, but one possible benchmark is the level of the primary balance that would be consistent with maintaining a constant public debt-to-GDP ratio in the context of low inflation and no financial repression. The existence of a potential credibility problem could be signaled by a path of the actual primary deficit that greatly exceeded this "sustainable" one, implying either a continued increase in the public sector debt-to-GDP ratio (and therefore a rising servicing burden) or the need for continued reliance on the inflation tax or financial repression (Chart 13).[27] In the latter case, the fiscal stance would be inconsistent with a low inflation objective or financial sector reform. The consistency with financial liberalization is important because a number of countries in the study (for example, India, Mexico, and Morocco) initially fi-

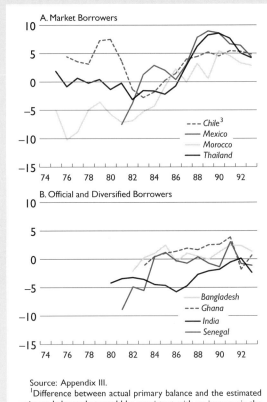

Chart 13. Difference Between Actual and "Sustainable" Fiscal Primary Balances[1,2]
(In percent of GDP)

Source: Appendix III.
[1]Difference between actual primary balance and the estimated primary balance that would be consistent with no increase in the government debt-to-GDP ratio, in the context of low inflation and no financial repression. A positive figure implies that the actual balance is above the sustainable level (see Appendix III).
[2]Primary balance includes grants.
[3]Figures for Chile include the quasi-fiscal deficit of the central bank.

nanced a large part of their deficits by requiring banks and other financial institutions to hold domestic government securities at below-market interest rates.[28] Therefore, the partial or complete liberalization of interest rates implemented in these countries had a substantial impact on the fiscal deficit. Details of the exercise are presented in Appendix III.

The results suggest that Thailand's fiscal stance was broadly sustainable from the very outset of adjustment, which probably contributed to the relatively rapid pace of the private investment response. Among the countries that began their adjustment with large or intermediate fiscal imbalances, all made some progress toward setting public debt on a

---

[27]Chart 13 distinguishes between predominantly market borrowers and other countries because when countries benefit from substantial concessional external financing a rising debt-to-GDP ratio would not necessarily signal a potential problem, provided the concessional assistance could be expected to continue over the medium term.

The assessment is based on whether fiscal policy was likely to be judged sustainable *at the time* it was adopted, rather than with the benefit of hindsight; the calculation effectively assumes static expectations about the future path of relevant variables.

---

[28]See, for example, the discussion on Morocco in Nsouli and others (1995).

more sustainable path, although in several cases (notably Morocco among those with large initial imbalances) such a position was not attained until several years into the adjustment period. Moreover, in a few countries some of the progress toward fiscal sustainability was subsequently reversed (notably in Ghana and India), which may have contributed to the delayed crowding in of private investment in these countries. Mexico is of particular interest because it achieved a decisive up-front shift to a more sustainable fiscal position, in the narrow sense used here, and maintained that position throughout the entire adjustment period; yet the crowding-in effects in the form of higher private investment were slow to materialize and were relatively weak, thereby exacerbating the initial recession. The reasons for this will be explored more fully in the next section, but the debt crisis itself—and the associated shift in net resource transfers—involved a major switch in public sector financing from external to domestic sources, which constrained the availability of financing for the private sector at least through the mid-1980s.

Judgments about the sustainability of fiscal policy based on a debt dynamics criterion however, do not necessarily imply that fiscal policy is consistent with other macroeconomic objectives, notably the avoidance of excessive external current account deficits. The linkages between the fiscal and external imbalances are difficult to quantify on an ex-ante basis, in view of possible shifts in private sector saving and investment behavior at a time of substantial changes in macroeconomic and structural policies. Consequently, the fiscal adjustment framework may need to include contingency provisions in case the private sector response diverges substantially from that expected. For example, the different fiscal policy responses to the surges in capital inflows that occurred late in the adjustment period of several of the countries illustrate that a narrow debt dynamics criterion may not be a sufficient guide to the stance of fiscal policy. For example, in Mexico, fiscal policy did not respond to the surge in capital inflows of the early 1990s and the associated sharp decline in private saving; the fiscal position (excluding privatization revenues) was, however, in surplus. In contrast, Thailand's fiscal policy was more explicitly countercyclical, despite its comfortable public debt position. These issues are taken up again in Section VII.

Consistency of Macroeconomic Policies

Even during the transition toward a more sustainable medium-term fiscal position, an inconsistent mix of macroeconomic policies may have adverse consequences for investment and output growth. The experience of the eight countries suggests that two difficult areas are the mix of monetary and fiscal

policies and the coordination of fiscal, exchange rate, and wage policies.

The Mix of Monetary and Fiscal Policies

When faced with a macroeconomic crisis and constraints on the immediate scope for fiscal action, policymakers often tend to rely excessively on contractionary monetary policies. Such tendencies are exacerbated when adjustment is delayed, and access to external financing is sharply curtailed. In such circumstances, even quite strong fiscal adjustment may involve higher public sector domestic borrowing and a consequent squeeze on private sector credit. In this section, the yardsticks used to assess the stringency of private sector credit conditions are (1) growth rates of real bank credit to the private sector, which will reflect both changes in the demand for, and the supply of, credit[29] and (2) the level of real domestic interest rates compared with the real SDR interest rate, as an indicator of international financial market conditions (Chart 14).[30]

If interest rates are not market determined, excessive fiscal borrowing would tend to crowd out the private sector through a direct reduction in the amount of credit allocated by the banking system. Ghana, in the period prior to the Economic Recovery Program, is such a case when access to external financing was reduced sharply (Chart 15). Although some modest fiscal adjustment took place during this time, the main burden seems to have fallen on private sector credit, which was squeezed substantially in real terms (Table 7). Another example is Mexico during 1983–87, when, despite substantial fiscal adjustment, the share of private sector credit in total credit and in GDP declined, because of portfolio constraints designed to channel a substantial proportion of bank lending to the public sector, which had virtually no access to external financing after the debt crisis. Similar influences appear to have been at work in Morocco in 1986–88. Of course, in all these cases, the high degree of macroeconomic uncertainty probably also dampened the demand for credit.

If interest rates are somewhat more flexible, public sector borrowing requirements may absorb a large share of loanable funds from domestic credit markets and exert upward pressure on real interest rates or reduce private sector access to bank credit in still segmented credit markets. This appears to have

---

[29]Real credit is measured in terms of the contemporaneous rate of inflation of the GDP deflator.

[30]Domestic and international interest rates may, however, diverge for reasons other than financial policies, such as exchange rate expectations, and differences in tax systems (see Bennett (1995)). Moreover, when the rate of inflation is high and variable, any measure of the real interest rate can only be approximate.

Chart 14. Real Interest Rates[1]
(In percent per annum)

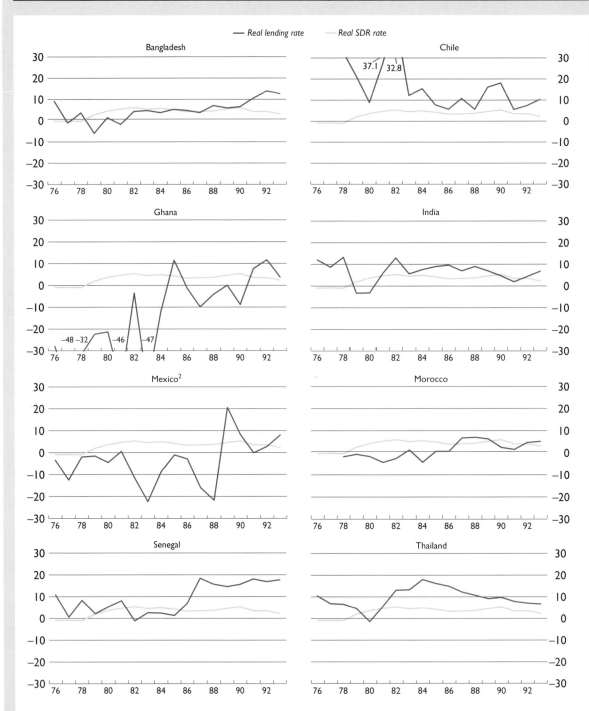

Sources: International Monetary Fund, *International Financial Statistics*; and IMF staff estimates.

[1]National nominal rates are deflated by the contemporaneous inflation rate of the GDP deflator. The real SDR rate is calculated as the weighted average interest rate on three-month instruments in the five countries whose currencies comprise the SDR deflated by the contemporaneous annual inflation rate of the GDP deflator. The weights are the currency units used in calculating the value of the SDR.

[2] Real deposit (not lending) rate.

Chart 15. Stock of Private Sector Credit[1]
(In percent of total domestic credit)

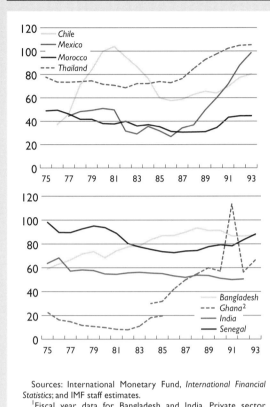

Sources: International Monetary Fund, *International Financial Statistics*; and IMF staff estimates.
[1]Fiscal year data for Bangladesh and India. Private sector includes public enterprises for Bangladesh, Morocco, and Senegal.
[2]Break in coverage of monetary accounts in 1984.

been an important factor in the early stages of the 1990–91 crisis in India, when the authorities had to rely primarily on monetary policy to restrain demand because of the political constraints on early fiscal action, which resulted in a sharp contraction in the volume of credit and a subsequent rise in interest rates. By contrast, the major fiscal consolidation in Thailand since 1987 contributed to a decline in real interest rates and the rapid rise in the share of private sector credit in total credit and in GDP.

A related issue is the problem of weak bank balance sheets and its implications for monetary policy. A high proportion of effectively nonperforming assets—although often not explicitly recognized as such—contributed to high interest margins and inefficient intermediation in a number of countries and appears to have been a major impediment to private investment in some (for example, Bangladesh). Be-

yond this, the continued extension of new credit to service bad loans, in a context of ineffective bank supervision, in some cases undermined the effectiveness of monetary policy in controlling aggregate demand and thereby contributed to the severity of the eventual crisis and recession. The starkest example of this is Chile prior to 1982 (see Section VIII).

Coordination of Fiscal, Exchange Rate, and Wage Policies

Perceived inconsistencies between exchange rate, wage, and fiscal policies may undermine the credibility of an adjustment program, increasing uncertainty and expectations of impending policy reversals. In such circumstances, adverse effects on investment and growth may materialize through upward pressures on real interest rates or on the real exchange rate. For example, given a predetermined path for the nominal exchange rate, a fiscal policy stance that fuels excess demand pressures risks leading to higher nontradable goods' prices and thereby an appreciated real exchange rate, with potentially penalizing effects on the contribution of net exports to growth. Equally important, continued backward-looking indexation practices limit the effectiveness of discrete exchange rate changes in bringing about a reduction in real wages and improvements in external competitiveness.

The influence of inconsistent fiscal and exchange rate policies appear to have been important in Mexico (1988–89) and Senegal (post-1987). In Mexico, interest rates rose sharply in the first year of the exchange-rate-based stabilization, reflecting incomplete credibility of the exchange rate anchor and large capital outflows. These pressures appear to have originated in part because of uncertainties surrounding the fiscal policy stance prior to the 1988 elections, as well as the shift to domestic debt financing of public sector borrowing requirements discussed earlier.[31] Moreover, in the later stages of the exchange-rate-based stabilization program (after 1992), the primary fiscal balance and public saving deteriorated. While it is doubtful that a strengthening of public finances sufficient to fully offset the impact of the massive capital inflows could have been feasible, a tighter fiscal stance could have helped to reduce the risks to external sustainability posed by the appreciation of the real exchange rate.

In Senegal, concern about the feasibility of the adjustment strategy led to a rise in the premiums on domestic over French franc interest rates after 1987. With a large persistent decline in the terms of trade,

---

[31]Real interest rates fell after a substantial increase in the primary fiscal surplus had been achieved and the Brady agreement for the restructuring of external debt was reached.

Table 7. Key Macroeconomic Indicators and Summary of Exchange Rate Policy
(In percent, unless otherwise specified; t refers to year in parentheses)

	Fiscal Deficit/GDP[1]		Primary Fiscal Deficit/GDP[1]		Average Change in Real Credit to Private Sector[2]	Change in Real Effective Exchange Rate[3]	Exchange Rate Policy
	t – 1	t + 2	t – 1	t + 2			
Bangladesh (1980/81)	–12	–11	...	...	12	–15	Adjustable peg. Dual exchange rate in effect.
Bangladesh (1985/86)	–7	–7	...	...	5	–19	Adjustable peg. Dual exchange rate unified in 1992.
Chile (1974)	–25[4]	—	...	2	55	—	Floating during 1974–77. During 1978–82, exchange-rate-based nominal anchor strategy, with a preannounced crawling rate at less than rate of inflation, followed by peg in 1980–82.
Chile[5] (1983)	–2	–2	–1	—	–3	–36	Substantial depreciation in 1983–84. Crawling band introduced in 1985, geared toward maintaining export competitiveness.
Ghana (1983)	–5	–3	–4	–2	30	–81	Series of large discrete devaluations to eliminate massive overvaluation. Parallel market premium reduced from 700 percent to 100 percent in 1986.
Ghana (1987)	–4	–4	–2	–2	–12	–30	Dual exchange rate system during 1986–90, with gradual unification since 1988. Managed floating since 1990.
India (1991/92)	–8	–8	–5	–3	—	–24	Peg with 19 percent devaluation in mid-1991. Managed floating since March 1993, with central bank intervention to dampen appreciation.
Mexico (1983)	–15	–8	–3	4	–5	5	Series of large discrete devaluations followed after 1986 by managed floating geared toward a real depreciation.
Mexico (1988)	–14	–2	6	8	16	36	Exchange-rate-based nominal anchor strategy: initial pegging (1988), followed by preannounced crawling rate at less than inflation rate. In November 1981, greater, albeit limited, flexibility with progressively wider intervention band. Floating rate after December 1994.
Morocco (1981)	–10	–12	–8	–7	5	–16	Adjustable peg with a series of devaluations through 1986 aimed at improving competitiveness.
Morocco (1986)	–10	–5	–3	2	–1	–11	Managed floating during late 1980s. Peg to a basket of currencies in 1990, following an initial devaluation. Small one-step devaluation in 1992.
Senegal (1985)	–6	–2	–2	—	1	12	Peg (CFA franc zone).
Senegal (1989)	–2	—	1	3	–1	–12	Peg (CFA franc zone); 50 percent devaluation in early 1994.
Thailand (1984)	–5	–5	–2	–2	9	–22	Adjustable peg with devaluations in 1981 (9 percent) and 1984 (15 percent).
Thailand (1987)	–5	3	–2	5	21	–7	Peg to an undisclosed basket of currencies. Weight of U.S. dollar increased in basket in late 1980s, resulting in nominal depreciation vis-a-vis many trading partners.

[1]Excluding grants.
[2]Average annual change over the three-year period (t through t + 2); deflated by GDP deflator. For Bangladesh, Morocco, and Senegal, includes credit to public enterprises.
[3]Percentage change in real effective exchange rate between (t – 1) and (t + 2). A minus sign indicates a depreciation.
[4]Revisions to national income accounts imply that ratios to GDP prior to 1975 may not be strictly comparable to later estimates.
[5]Fiscal deficits excluding central bank losses.

fiscal and public sector wage policy (especially in the early 1990s when the fiscal deficit increased and arrears were accumulated) became inconsistent with the fixed parity between the CFA franc and the French franc.[32]

Labor market and fiscal policies were also crucial in determining the trade-off in exchange-rate-based disinflation programs between inflation reduction and a loss of external competitiveness; both sides of this trade-off have potential implications for growth.[33] This is illustrated by the examples of Mexico (post-1988) and Chile (1978–82). In Mexico, the exchange rate anchor was supported by successive forward-looking wage-price "pacts" agreed upon with the private sector, which succeeded, at least partially, in breaking inflation inertia.[34] However, the real exchange rate did subsequently appreciate, under pressure from capital inflows and labor market policies that provided inadequate support for the exchange rate anchor (see also Section VIII). By contrast, in Chile (1978–82) there was no attempt to change the existing system of full backward-looking wage indexation during the preannounced nominal exchange rate period. This inconsistency contributed to excess demand pressures and a real exchange rate

appreciation. In these circumstances, high interest rates reflected widespread expectations of an impending devaluation as well as private sector over-borrowing to finance purchases of imported goods that culminated in an unsustainable deterioration of the external current account.

In contrast, the potential benefits of coordinated exchange rate, fiscal, and labor market policies for providing adequate incentives to the tradable goods sector and eliciting a strong resource-switching response are well illustrated by the later adjustment episode in Chile and by Thailand. Chile's strong recovery after 1984 owed much to the sustained real depreciation of the exchange rate that underpinned a sharp increase in the volume of exports other than of copper. The success with which nominal exchange rate depreciations were translated into a significant real depreciation reflected the suspension of compulsory wage indexation in 1982 and the large fiscal retrenchment. The persistence of considerable unemployment at least until 1987 was also an important factor in holding real wages in check. In Thailand, depreciation of the nominal exchange rate contributed to a large sustained real depreciation after 1984 and induced large export market gains. The magnitude of the real depreciation closely matched the size of the nominal devaluation reflecting the flexibility of Thailand's labor market, a tradition of relatively low inflation, and stable macroeconomic policies that kept inflationary expectations in check. The achievement of sizable fiscal surpluses helped contain inflationary pressures when economic activity surged and offset upward pressures on the exchange rate stemming from large capital inflows.

---

[32] Public sector wages were an important benchmark for formal sector wages. See Tahari and others (forthcoming).

[33] The comparison of Chile (1974–75) with Mexico (1987) also illustrates the influence of the nominal anchor choice on the timing of any downturn in economic activity associated with the disinflation strategy: money-based disinflation programs are typically associated with an early downturn and exchange-rate-based programs with a late recession. See Calvo and Végh (1992 and 1993), Kiguel and Liviatan (1992), and Rebelo and Végh (1995).

[34] See, for example, Edwards (1993).

V Private Investment

The cross-country evidence discussed in Section III confirmed that the absence of a stable environment for economic decision making is an important impediment to private investment. Yet progress toward macroeconomic stability has sometimes proved insufficient to generate a rapid recovery of investment. Lags, at times long and protracted, in the response of private investment have raised concerns on possible links between the design of adjustment policies and the duration of these lags. The rate of domestic saving may also have influenced the pace of the recovery in investment, especially when access to international capital markets was limited.[35]

The experience of the eight countries reveals marked differences in the response of private investment to adjustment policies—in terms of the steepness of the initial decline, whether there was an identifiable period of "pause" before recovery began,[36] and the magnitude of the observed recovery (see Table 4 and Chart 7). The record of falling private investment rates in the early years of adjustment ranged from a precipitous drop in Chile during the 1982–83 crisis (following an unsustainable boom fueled by expectations of a devaluation) to smaller, but still substantial, declines observed in India, Mexico, Morocco, and Thailand. Comparison of program targets with actual outcomes suggests that, on average, targets under IMF-supported programs for the eight countries were generally too sanguine about the prospects for an early rebound in private investment (Box 2).

A marked investment pause—lasting three to four years—occurred in two countries: Mexico during the first adjustment period and Morocco in 1985–88. In Ghana, private investment rose when the Economic Recovery Program was introduced, although the initial rebound suffered a brief hiccup in 1986. Private investment in Bangladesh and Senegal was persistently flat with minor fluctuations around low rates in the range of 5 percent to 10 percent of GDP. For these two countries, the record points to a protracted stagnation, rather than a simple postadjustment pause of investment, suggesting that structural impediments were especially important (see Section VIII).[37]

As for the strength of the subsequent recovery, when it existed three groups can be identified: (1) a weak, uneven recovery in Ghana and Morocco; (2) a delayed, but significant recovery in Mexico to investment rates around 15 percent of GDP; and (3) a stronger, more rapid recovery to investment rates in excess of 20 percent of GDP (in Chile) or 30 percent of GDP (in Thailand).

With this background, three questions are addressed in this section. First, does the gradual response of investment observed in many of the countries come as a surprise or should a lag be expected on the basis of rational economic behavior? Second, what is the empirical evidence on the role of public policies in influencing the observed pattern of private investment? Third, how can the lag in the investment response be minimized and the recovery accelerated?

Factors Affecting the Lagged Response of Private Investment

In general, a certain lag in the response of private investment during or after a period of adjustment should be expected based on the theory of investment behavior. Such a lag could reflect the rational response of private investors to adjustment costs or to uncertainty about the permanence of changes in macroeconomic and structural policies, as well as the more conventional effects stemming from demand management policies.

The considerations emerging from investment studies (Box 3) suggest that the perceived credibility

---

[35]The causality between investment and saving (and growth) can, however, operate in both directions.

[36]The concept of investment pause is used here and in recent studies (Serven and Solimano (1994)) to indicate the reaching of a plateau after the initial decline, during which period neither a noticeable recovery nor a further decline takes place. The length of the pause cannot be simply equated to the time between a peak investment rate and the subsequent return to that rate because the initial peak could be associated with unsustainable macroeconomic conditions, as in Chile or Mexico prior to the 1982 crisis.

[37]Private investment in India during the 1970s and most of the 1980s followed a similar pattern.

Box 2. Investment: Program Targets and Outcomes

IMF-supported programs for the eight countries have, on average, experienced only small shortfalls between targeted and actual investment rates, with most of the shortfall occurring in the early program years.[1] However, targets for private investment in the initial program year appear on average to have been too optimistic.

In the initial program year, the ratio of total investment to GDP was targeted, on average, to rise slightly, whereas the actual outcome was a small decline; the average shortfall was 0.4 percentage point of GDP (see chart). The shortfall for private investment was almost 1 percentage point of GDP. On average, programs targeted a pickup in private investment in the initial year, whereas actual investment changed little, suggesting that programs for the eight countries typically took insufficient account of the tendency for private investment to respond to adjustment with a lag. The shortfall was partly offset by public investment, which declined by less than targeted.[2] Differences between targets and actuals for the second and third program years were generally smaller, with the main shortfalls occurring in public investment.

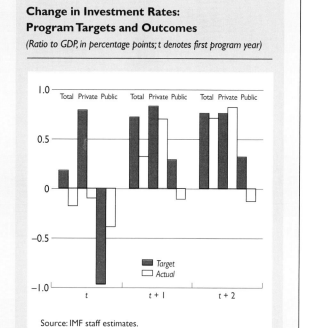

Change in Investment Rates: Program Targets and Outcomes

(Ratio to GDP, in percentage points; t denotes first program year)

Source: IMF staff estimates.

---

[1]The sample covers initial targets in programs supported by stand-by arrangements under the upper credit tranches, the structural adjustment facility, and the enhanced structural adjustment facility. In contrast, for the 36 countries covered in the last review of IMF conditionality (Schadler and others (1995)) there was, on average, no shortfall in investment for programs covered by that review.

[2]Since not all programs contain a breakdown between targets for public and private investment, differences in sample coverage mean the components do not add up to the total.

---

of public policies is important in orienting private investors' decisions. Indeed, if investors perceive that relative prices are highly uncertain, and policy measures poorly coordinated or likely to be reversed, they may delay committing resources until a more positive assessment is possible. Also, since firms have incomplete information and may in practice gauge investment prospects partly by observing competitors' and partners' behavior, the economy may get locked into a low-investment and low-growth equilibrium if a sufficient number of firms postpone investment. In contrast, policies perceived as consistent and unlikely to be reversed may turn expectations around and induce a positive response of private investors, thereby reducing the costs of adjustment.

Determinants of Investment and the Role of Public Policies

In order to examine the relative importance of these effects in the eight countries, econometric estimates of the determinants of investment combined traditional neoclassical influences with factors specific to developing countries and indicators of uncertainty and macrostability.[38] The results are summarized in Table 8 and presented in more detail in Appendix IV. The impact of individual factors on the decline, pause, or recovery of private investment varies. Table 9 provides a summary of the salient in-

---

[38]The dependent variable was the share of private (or nongovernment) investment in GDP. The estimated equations included as determinants: (1) the growth of aggregate economic activity, lagged to reduce simultaneity problems; (2) financial variables, notably real interest rates and the volume of credit to the private sector; (3) public investment, to assess complementarity versus substitutability with private investment; (4) the availability of foreign exchange; (5) proxies for uncertainty (volatility of selected macro variables) and other indicators of macroeconomic instability such as inflation and debt and debt-service ratios; and (6) measures of external shocks. In general, the equations tracked private investment developments reasonably well, albeit with noticeable differences in goodness of fit—as the adjusted R-squared ranged from 0.6 to 0.9 across countries. The comparability of results is complicated by differences in the treatment of public enterprise investment, which is included in the dependent variable in the cases of Chile and Senegal.

Box 3. What Does the Literature Say About Lags in Investment?

Studies of private investment behavior emphasize two complementary factors—the existence of costs to adjusting the capital stock and the role of uncertainty and irreversibility—in order to explain the lagged response of investment to changes in policies and incentives. These factors suggest caution in assuming a strong response of private capital formation in the early stages of an adjustment program.

If costs related to the purchase and installation of capital increase with the investment rate, they create incentives for a gradual transition from actual to desired levels of capital.[1] However, these costs can be influenced by policies. In particular, the transition period may be unduly protracted by credit-rationing constraints and structural problems of financial intermediaries; by the large weight of the public sector, often hampering private initiative with distortions and regulations; or by constraints on access to foreign exchange or financing for imported capital goods.

The timing of private investment decisions may also be affected by uncertainty and irreversibility effects.[2] An increase in uncertainty causes risk-averse firms to reallocate resources away from risky activities, thereby lowering the desired stock of capital.[3] Also, if the outcomes of irreversible investments turn out to be worse than expected, risk-neutral investors may get stuck with low returns, whereas if prospects improve new entrants may compete away part of the gains. Consequently, downside risk may increase without corresponding upside gain, so that waiting may have value as it gives firms the opportunity to process new information before committing resources.[4] The role of these factors however is hard to test empirically because the available indicators—such as measures of volatility of inflation or other relevant variables—may only partially capture the impact of policy uncertainty.

_____

[2]Irreversibility arises from sunk costs related to firm-specific investment and the large discount in valuing secondhand equipment.

[3]Inflation uncertainty may also lower investment by obscuring price signals, and credit rationing may intensify as uncertainty increases.

[4]See Dixit (1992), Dixit and Pindyck (1994), and Pindyck (1991).

_____

[1]Costs related to the purchase, delivery, and installation of new capital goods play a central role in the dynamic response of investment in both the neoclassical theory and in Tobin's q theory of investment.

fluences behind major investment episodes in each country, drawing upon both the econometric and other evidence in the country case studies. Several broad conclusions emerge.

Effects from lagged economic activity played an important role in most countries except Bangladesh. In Chile, Ghana, India, Mexico, and Thailand[39] these effects were strongly significant, less so in Morocco and Senegal. This implies that any contractionary effects of adjustment policies on output would have a short-run impact on private investment. However, this variable may also act as a channel of transmission for confidence effects and private sector expectations, which can be influenced, for instance, by protracted financial imbalances and measures affecting perceptions of the pro-business orientation of policies. Such influences appear to have been especially important in Mexico and Chile prior to and during the debt crisis.

High real interest rates and constraints on the growth of credit to the private sector contributed in several instances to a decline or slowed the recovery of investment (Bangladesh, India, Mexico, and

Thailand).[40] As discussed in the preceding section, both the effects of the mix of monetary and fiscal policies, as well as the impact of structural problems in the financial sector, were contributing factors in several cases.[41] The results suggest that greater efforts to improve competition and efficiency of financial intermediaries and to ensure an adequate flow of credit to the private sector could have yielded a stronger investment response. There were, however, episodes where sharply increasing real rates did not prevent investment from rising. For example, in Chile the private sector spending spree on imported consumption and investment goods prior to the 1982

_____

[39]For Thailand, economic activity in partner countries was a major influence on private investment, suggesting that the investment boom that began in the second half of the 1980s was due in part to broader regional developments.

[40]The initial specification of investment equations included both credit volumes—capturing credit rationing effects—and real interest rates since in several instances restrictions affecting both quantities and prices in the market for credit were in place for at least part of the sample. Constraints on the availability of credit proved important in India, Mexico, and less so in Bangladesh and Morocco, while proxies for the user cost of capital—that is, real ex-post interest rates or the relative price of capital goods—were significant in most cases except Senegal. In countries adopting financial liberalization reforms (Mexico, for example) the influence of interest rates gained greater prominence over time.

[41]In particular, the weak response of private investment in Bangladesh appears to have been caused in part by increasing bank spreads and credit rationing, indicating a problem of weak bank balance sheets.

Table 8. Selected Factors Influencing Private Investment[1]

Country	Sample Period	Endogenous Variable: Share of Investment in GDP	Aggregate activity (Lagged growth of real GDP)	Financial variables		Public Investment (Share in GDP)	Measures of uncertainty / macroeconomic instability			
				Real interest rate/ relative price	Real growth of credit to private sector		Inflation rate/parallel market premium/ real effective exchange rate	External debt/debt service	Sample volatility measures (or other)	External shocks
Bangladesh	1979/80–1993/94	Private, constant prices	NS	– –	+	NS		– – –	– – –	
Chile	1975–93	Nongovernment, constant prices	+++	– –	NS	– – –	NS	– – –	NS	NS
Ghana	1971–93	Private, current prices	+++	– –	NS	– – –	– – –	NS	NS	++
India	1973/74–1993/94	Private, constant prices	+++[2]	–	+	– – –		– – –	– – –	
Mexico	1972–93	Private, current prices	+++	–	++	– – –	NS	NS	–	NS
	1981–93	Private, constant prices	++	– – –	++	–	– – –		NS	
Morocco	1972–93	Private, constant prices	+	– –	+	+++	– – –	NS	NS	++[3] –[4]
Senegal	1978–93	Nongovernment, constant prices	+	NS	NS	– – –	– – –	– – –	[5]	NS
Thailand	1970–93	Private, constant prices	+++[6]	–		– – –	– – –	NS	NS	NS

Source: Appendix IV, Table 18.

[1]Sign of the estimated coefficient: +, – = not statistically significant at 5 percent level, but significant at a marginally higher level; ++, – – = statistically significant at 5 percent; +++, – – – = statistically significant at 1 percent; NS indicates not statistically significant and not retained in final preferred specification; blank cells indicate variables omitted in individual countries.

[2]Lagged growth in industrial production.

[3]Export price shock (in percent of GDP).

[4]Import price shock (in percent of GDP).

[5]Government domestic borrowing requirement including involuntary accumulation of arrears (in percent of GDP).

[6]Real GDP growth in partner countries.

Table 9. Summary of Main Factors Explaining Major Episodes of Private Investment Performance[1]

Country	Investment Performance (Corresponding period)	Main Reasons
Bangladesh	Prolonged stagnation and weak recovery (1980–93)	Weak financial sector and large nonperforming loans leading to high interest rate spreads Administrative and regulatory impediments Macroeconomic policy uncertainty in early 1980s
Chile[2]	Sharp decline (1981–83)	Severe recession associated with financial crisis and external shocks Weak financial sector balance sheets
	Strong recovery (1983–93)	Sustained recovery in economic activity Substantial improvements in external debt-service profile Successful structural reforms
Ghana	Uneven, weak recovery (1983–91)	Persistent macroeconomic policy uncertainty Weak financial sector balance sheets Crowding-out effects of public investment
India	Overall flat trend followed by decline (1990/91–1992/93)	Cost and availability of credit Crowding-out effects of public investment prior to 1990/91 Slowdown of industrial production beginning in 1990/91 Uncertainty associated with greater volatility of inflation beginning in 1990/91 Continued regulatory impediments despite substantial reform
Mexico	Decline (1981–83)	Recession associated with financial crisis and external shocks Severe erosion of private sector confidence in public policies Sharp contraction of credit to the private sector
	Pause (1983–87)	Persistent macroeconomic instability (high inflation) Stagnating economic activity Uncertainty due to unresolved external debt situation and weak private sector confidence
	Moderate recovery (1987–93)	Progress in macroeconomic stability and disinflation Progress in private sector access to bank credit through financial reform Confidence effects from resolution of external debt problem (acting through interest rates, although these remained high for part of the period)
Morocco	Decline (1982–85)	Reduction of complementary public investment Rising real interest rates and higher cost of imported capital goods
	Pause (1985–88) and weak, uneven recovery (1989–93)	Reduction of complementary public investment Rising real interest rates Slow growth of economic activity (supply shocks) Higher costs of imported capital goods

Table 9 (concluded)

Country	Investment Performance (Corresponding period)	Main Reasons
Senegal[2]	Flat trend	Weak external competitiveness Rising external debt in early 1980s Crowding-out effects of public investment Persistence of structural distortions
Thailand	Strong recovery (1986–93)	Decline in relative unit labor costs; and strong demand in partner countries Macroeconomic stability Pro-business orientation of policies

Source: IMF staff estimates.
[1]Based on econometric estimates and additional evidence from country case studies.
[2]Nongovernment investment.

crisis occurred in the context of a sharp rise in real lending rates.[42]

Uncertainty and macroeconomic instability—captured by a variety of indicators in individual country estimates—exerted adverse and strongly significant effects on private capital formation. These factors appear to have been especially important in Mexico, where persistent, high inflation was an important deterrent to real private investment during the 1983–87 pause; in Ghana, where parallel market premiums captured the lingering impact of foreign exchange controls and slippages in financial policies induced the 1992–93 investment decline; and in Senegal, where inflation and rising external debt contributed to hold back nongovernment investment in the early 1980s.

However, there are also indications that broader confidence factors associated with internal and external financial crises had a major influence on the turning points of the investment cycle. In Mexico, the depth and speed of the investment decline in the aftermath of the 1982 crisis were sharper than predicted by the estimated investment equation and probably reflected the erosion of confidence in public policies due to the partial default on domestic debt, the imposition of exchange controls, and the nationalization of the banking system. In Chile, the sharp decline of nongovernment investment in 1981–83 was also linked to a severe financial crisis. In this case, major problems were the large external debt burden, the perceived inconsistency between exchange rate and wage policies, the associated private sector overspending, and the precarious condition of the financial system.

As for the role of public investment, evidence for the eight countries provides little support for the view that private and aggregate public investment are complementary. In six countries, the effect of public investment was found to be negative and strongly significant, implying that public investment competed with and crowded out private sector opportunities. The exceptions were Bangladesh, where no effect was detected, and Morocco where the two were largely complementary.[43] In countries where there was evidence of a negative overall relationship between public and private investment, efforts to rationalize and better select public investment programs and associated privatization reforms appear to have been instrumental in promoting, rather than hampering, private investment. However, this is an area where generalizations are difficult, as shown by the different results reported in the empirical literature.[44]

[42]Estimates of the impact of real lending rates on investment proved insignificant in the case of Chile. Expectations of an imminent devaluation and continued lending in support of nonperforming loans appear to have been the dominant factors prior to the 1982 crisis.

[43]In Morocco, the complementarity effects were strongest in the 1980s when the reduction in the share of government investment may have contributed to the pause and weak recovery of private investment. Crowding-out effects appear to have been stronger during the period of rapid public investment expansion in the 1970s.
[44]For example, Easterly, Rodríguez, and Schmidt-Hebbel (1994) found that crowding-out effects predominated in about half of the countries covered, whereas earlier cross-country studies (Serven and Solimano (1994)) found complementarity between public and private investment. Also, estimates of investment equations in the country case studies indicate that crowding-out effects may vary in strength over time. The discussion in the companion study (Mackenzie and others (forthcoming)) points to some evidence suggesting that public infrastructure investment (in particular investment in transport and communication) may complement private sector investment.

Also, several qualifications are in order. First, lack of data prevented addressing the important distinction between infrastructural and noninfrastructural public investment.[45] While Chile, Mexico, and Thailand made progress in enhancing the role of the private sector in utilities and infrastructural projects, in Thailand the cautious public investment policies resulted in infrastructural bottlenecks by the early 1990s. Second, while the rationalization of public investment programs created opportunities for the private sector, the associated reduction of demand affected private investment indirectly. Third, the efficiency of public investment, and hence its full impact on growth, cannot be deduced from the aggregate relationships discussed here.[46]

How Can Policies Accelerate the Response of Private Investment?

Experience in the eight countries suggests a number of conclusions:

• Achievement of greater macroeconomic stability was conducive to private investment. Progress in reducing inflation (Mexico and Senegal) and the parallel market premium (Ghana), in keeping the external debt-servicing burden under check (Chile, Bangladesh, and Senegal), in avoiding excessive real exchange rate appreciations and maintaining real wage flexibility (Thailand and Morocco) all helped promote conditions conducive to higher private investment rates. However, the magnitude of each effect varied across countries and over time.

• Uncertainty about the course of policies appears to have penalized private investment. Therefore,

avoidance of measures adversely affecting private sector confidence in public policies, clear announcement signals, and sustained implementation of mutually consistent policies are likely to reinforce credibility and reduce lags in the response of investors.

• Except for Morocco, there is no evidence that the reduction of public investment had negative effects on private investment. Rather, the estimates indicate that, in terms of direct contemporaneous links, substitutability effects dominated in most of the countries, suggesting that efforts to rationalize public investment programs create opportunities for private investment. This does not mean specific public investments, especially in infrastructure or human capital development, are not essential to support higher private investment and growth. Nor does it say how squeezing public investments during fiscal adjustment would affect growth; indeed, it is difficult to answer such a question without detailed cost-benefit analyses. However, it does question the wisdom of a general, untargeted increase in public capital spending as a way to elicit a faster private investment response.

• The findings suggest that ensuring an adequate flow of credit to the private sector, including through the removal of credit constraints when they are in place, is likely to promote a faster recovery of investment. Both an inappropriate mix of monetary and fiscal policies and structural problems in the financial sector can reduce private investment. The experience of Bangladesh also suggests that easing financial repression and lifting administrative restrictions may not by themselves be sufficient to ease credit constraints if the latter stem from an inherited stock of nonperforming assets. Furthermore, increasing competition in the banking system and addressing macroeconomic and structural problems that contribute to poorly performing portfolios may reduce the incidence of excessive bank spreads and high real lending rates. The importance of removing structural distortions affecting financial intermediation and the allocation of resources is underscored by the experience of countries with a relatively flat investment record, all of which showed lagging progress in these areas.

---

[45]A distinction between infrastructure and other public investment was possible for India. When both variables were included in the investment equation, they had negative signs although the infrastructure term was not statistically significant.

[46]For India, estimates of real rates of return to different categories of investment suggest that public sector investments in manufacturing have yielded much lower rates of return than either public infrastructural investment or private investment in manufacturing.

VI Saving

ost empirical evidence suggests that there is a strong and robust positive correlation between the rate of national saving and GDP growth.[47] Although the direction of causality is a debated issue, saving and growth are likely to reinforce each other, resulting in a virtuous circle for countries that are successful in achieving a sustained increase in saving.[48] Appropriate policies can help achieve such a result. An improvement in public saving appears to be the most effective policy instrument for increasing national saving, despite some partial offset in private saving.[49] But conventional measures of public saving can be misleading, since they tend to exclude a substantial share of expenditures devoted to human capital accumulation. For example, fiscal consolidation that raised measured public saving at the expense of reduced current spending on primary education would be likely to harm growth prospects.[50] Other potential policy-related influences on private saving include changes in taxation;[51] interest rates; changes in the severity of liquidity constraints; and the possible redistributive effects of devaluation (from labor income to profits) if the propensity to save out of profits is higher. However, it has generally been difficult to identify many of these effects empirically for developing countries.

Evidence of the Links Between Policies and Saving

Panel data estimates from an IMF staff study provide some indications of the influences at work in the countries of the present study.[52] In addition to reaffirming that an increase in public saving tends to be associated with higher national saving, the estimates also suggest that a decrease in the dependency ratio raised private saving substantially and that increases in per capita income raised private saving rates in developing countries. Changes in real interest rates had no significant effect on private or national saving. Increases in foreign saving affected national saving negatively; the offset was only partial, estimated to be between 40 percent and 50 percent, suggesting that an increased availability of external financing typically supports both higher consumption and higher investment. Finally, terms of trade windfalls were found to have a positive, but transitory, effect on national saving.

The estimated equations were able to track the path of saving reasonably well for most of the countries of the present study, suggesting that the above explanatory variables account for much of the variation in saving in these cases. However, the actual decline in national saving in Mexico beginning in the late 1980s and the substantial increase in Chile and Thailand during the same period were both considerably larger than predicted.[53]

---

[47]Empirical evidence on the determinants of saving was discussed in Savastano (1995) and Masson and others (1995).

[48]There is also considerable evidence that saving rates rise with per capita income levels, especially during the transition from low income levels once subsistence needs are satisfied; see Ogaki and others (1996).

[49]Empirical studies generally reject full Ricardian equivalence (a proposition implying that changes in public saving lead to equal and offsetting changes in private saving), but find that an increase in public saving results in a partial offset in private saving. Estimates of the offset coefficient are typically in the 0.4–0.6 range; see Savastano (1995) and Corbo and Schmidt-Hebbel (1991).

[50]The issue is also complicated by the difficulty of distinguishing between the inputs (that is, spending) and outputs of the government sector and by intergenerational concerns (for example, changes in unfunded pension liabilities). See International Monetary Fund, Fiscal Affairs Department (1995).

[51]Taxes affect saving by altering the rate of return enjoyed by savers. The evidence on the impact of taxes on saving, discussed in the companion study (see Mackenzie and others (forthcoming)), is that tax policy probably does not have a marked effect on the total but can affect substantially its composition. Tax schemes favoring particular classes of saving can entail substantial distortions.

---

[52]Masson and others (1995); the panel data covered 64 developing countries over the period 1970–93, and included all countries of the present study except Senegal.

[53]Hadjimichael and Ghura (1995) used a panel of 41 sub-Saharan African countries (including Ghana and Senegal) over 1986–92 to investigate the effectiveness of public policies in stimulating private saving and investment. They found that policies that kept inflation low, reduced macroeconomic uncertainty, promoted financial deepening, and increased public saving were conducive to higher national saving. They also found that policies leading to a reduction in the external debt burden significantly increased measured national saving.

Chart 16. National Saving Rates[1]
(In percent of GDP)

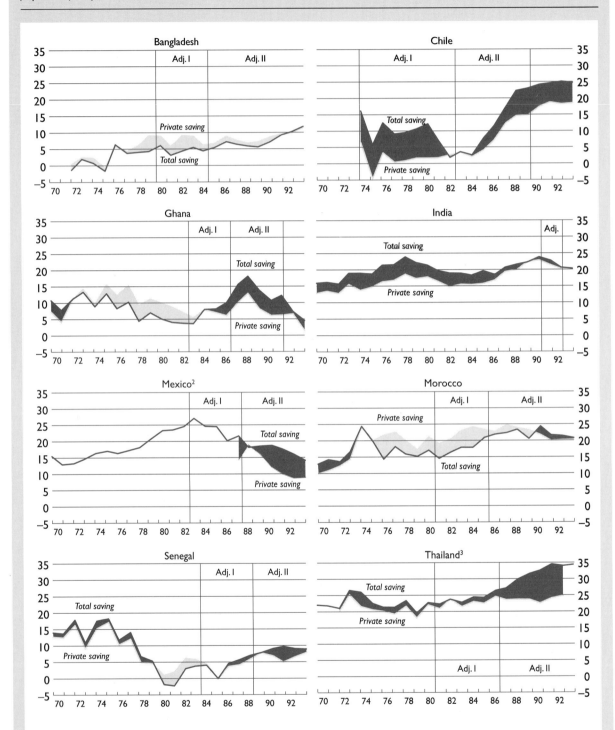

Sources: IMF staff estimates except data for Mexico, 1970–86, which are from International Monetary Fund, *World Economic Outlook*, various issues.

[1] Heavily shaded areas represent positive public saving, while lighter shading represents negative public saving.

[2] Separate data for private and public saving in Mexico prior to 1987 are not available.

[3] Separate data for private and public saving in Thailand in 1970, 1971, and 1993 are not available.

Evidence for Individual Countries

Developments in saving in the eight countries can be summarized as follows (Chart 16).[54]

---

[54] Data limitations complicate the analysis of saving, which is typically measured as a residual and is beset by classification, valuation, and measurement problems. Public saving data for

- In most countries, the national saving rate typically declined prior to adjustment as a result of expansionary policies that led to a fall in public saving,

---

Bangladesh, Chile, India, and Thailand include that of public enterprises; in the four other countries, public enterprise saving is included with that of the private sector.

Box 4. Saving: Program Targets and Outcomes

Most IMF-supported programs in the eight countries aimed for an increase in saving, but this failed to materialize in about half of the cases.[1] Part of the shortfall seems to be accounted for by interactions between public and private saving that were different than assumed under the programs. Thus, in over half of the years covered, increases in both public and private saving were programmed, whereas actual outcomes were more in line with the empirically observed tendency for increases in public saving to be partially offset by a fall in private saving (see chart). The largest shortfalls occurred in Mexico (see discussion in main text).

---

[1] Data cover IMF-supported programs in the eight countries during 1980–93; for multiyear programs, the initial program targets are used for all years.

One should avoid drawing direct conclusions on the effectiveness or consistency of IMF-supported programs on the basis of this data. Exogenous shocks influenced the outcomes; moreover, observed empirical associations hold over a longer time period than that of IMF-supported programs, and variable lags can affect the contemporaneous associations, especially following periods of serious macroeconomic imbalances. Nevertheless, this exercise highlights the need to pay more attention to the implicit assumptions on private saving and its interaction with public saving, when formulating program targets for the external current account and fiscal and monetary policies. Evidence presented in Savastano (1995) suggests there was little shortfall, on average, in total national saving in the more recent programs that were covered by the last review of IMF conditionality (Schadler and others (1995)).

Saving: Targets and Outcomes
(In percent of GDP)

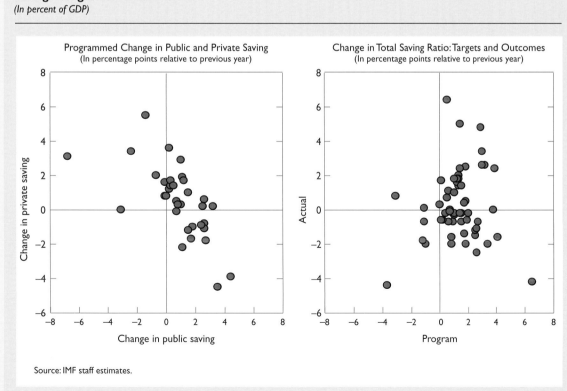

Source: IMF staff estimates.

or of consumption smoothing, or both in the face of adverse terms of trade shocks.

- Several countries (Bangladesh, Ghana, Senegal, and Morocco) achieved a moderate increase in saving rates during adjustment, although the gain was short-lived for Ghana.[55]
- Only two countries (Chile and Thailand) achieved large and lasting increases in national saving rates, suggesting a shift to a path where higher saving and higher growth are mutually reinforcing.
- In marked contrast, saving rates in Mexico declined substantially during the second adjustment period.

How did policies contribute to these developments? Evidence from the country studies and Masson and others (1995) suggests that, in most cases, higher public saving was a major factor behind the increases in saving during the adjustment periods. However, non-policy-related factors also played a substantial role in a number of countries—notably the large fluctuations in the terms of trade as well as supply shocks in Ghana, Morocco, and Senegal.

Did specific aspects of the design of policies in Thailand and Chile contribute to their especially favorable saving performance? In Thailand, the only unusual factor was the size of the increase in public saving—to over 10 percent of GDP by the early 1990s—as part of a deliberate policy choice to offset demand pressures arising from capital inflows. Private saving was also buoyant, but country-specific econometric studies suggest that, rather than any policies designed specifically to promote higher private saving, the main factors were the beneficial effects of rapid real income growth, the favorable macroeconomic environment, as well as demographic changes associated with a large decline in the dependency ratio.[56]

Chile did implement a comprehensive set of policy measures in the 1980s designed to boost the national saving rate. The improvement in public saving brought about by the major fiscal adjustment and the reduction of central bank losses was reinforced by the funneling of increased export earnings from the copper price boom of the late 1980s into the Copper Stabilization Fund. Public enterprise reforms, including large-scale privatization and a hardening of budget constraints, raised enterprise profitability and also reduced the drain on the budget.[57] A major pen-

sion reform began in 1981, involving a shift to a fully privatized saving plan and an increase in the retirement age. The initial impact of the reform was to reduce public saving and increase private saving; in addition, the reform was a major factor in deepening the capital market.[58] Finally, important income tax reforms, designed specifically to increase saving through reduced rate progressivity and various incentives were implemented in 1984, but their impact on saving is difficult to assess.

The case of Mexico illustrates the potential for sizable unanticipated effects on private saving behavior as a result of changes in macroeconomic and structural policies. These effects can be especially large if there is some doubt about the consistency and sustainability of policies at the same time that financial sector liberalization and capital inflows ease liquidity constraints. In fact, program targets for private, and hence total, saving under the 1989–92 extended arrangement with the IMF were missed by wide margins.[59] More generally, whereas most IMF-supported programs in the eight countries targeted an increase in saving, this did not occur in about half of the programs (Box 4). Although the causes of the saving decline in Mexico are not yet well established, several factors may have been responsible. The initial decline in 1988 resulted from a consumption boom fueled by purchases of imported durables that may have been brought forward because of doubts about the sustainability of the announced exchange rate anchor. But it is unlikely that this can explain the prolonged nature of the decline. Rather, there are indications that substantial capital inflows at a time of financial market liberalization eased consumers' liquidity constraints.[60]

---

[55]The reversal of the saving gains in Ghana during the early 1990s reflected, in part, fiscal policy slippages that led to lower public saving.

[56]See, for example, Faruqee and Husain (1995).

[57]The Chilean privatization program resulted in a large reclassification of firms from the public to private sector, which complicates judgments on the relative contributions of each sector to the improvement in national saving. Partial write-offs of private sector domestic debt also complicate the estimates.

[58]The privatized plans contributed the equivalent of 2–3 percentage points of GDP to national saving throughout the 1980s; the net impact is harder to estimate because of reduced saving elsewhere, especially in the public sector. Bosworth and others (1994) contains a detailed discussion of the reform.

[59]At the start of the extended arrangement, a cumulative improvement in private saving of about 1 percentage point of GDP was targeted for 1989–92, whereas the eventual outcome was a cumulative decline of 10 percentage points. Shortfalls from the revised targets prepared under each annual segment of the arrangement were also very large.

[60]In addition, the progress in reducing inflation and the resulting drop in the inflation tax, as well as completion of the Brady debt consolidation deal in late 1989, probably raised expected permanent incomes. The possible factors behind the decline in Mexico's private saving are discussed at greater length in Savastano (1995).

VII   Role of External Financing

An increased availability of external financing during adjustment can facilitate growth by financing higher investment, helping to avoid sharp declines in domestic absorption or imports, and improving confidence by bolstering reserves or resolving arrears problems. Whether these effects occur in practice will depend importantly upon the response of policies. The interaction between policies and financing is complex, and it has typically been difficult to identify a robust association between external financing and growth from cross-country or time-series studies.[61] As an illustration, the correlations between changes in net external financing and growth for the eight countries in the present study, and for a broader set of developing countries, were positive but rather small.[62] Moreover, the level of financing is itself likely to be an endogenous outcome, heavily influenced by a country's macroeconomic and structural policies. Causation probably acts in both directions, since faster growth may also attract capital inflows, including foreign direct investment.

Whether an increase in foreign saving is available to finance higher investment will depend upon how much is offset by lower domestic saving. Changes in net external financing appear to be positively associated (although not one-to-one) with changes in investment rates;[63] in this respect, the experience of

the eight countries appears to be broadly similar to that of developing countries in general (Chart 17).[64]

Examining particular episodes where the sharpest swings in net financing occurred in the eight countries highlights a number of further observations (Chart 18 and Table 10). Three types of episodes are considered here: countries that experienced severe debt crises and a cutoff in external financing; countries that benefited at some stage from a substantial pickup in official financing; and countries that have received substantial private capital inflows in recent years.

First, the earlier discussion has already indicated that delaying adjustment until forced by a sharp withdrawal of external financing is likely to be particularly costly, in terms of lower investment and output. The external borrowing constraints were most severe in countries that experienced major debt-servicing difficulties, with Mexico especially hard hit, despite the cushioning effects of exceptional financing from the IMF and World Bank. The estimated investment equations discussed earlier suggest that confidence factors associated with the debt crisis and the authorities' initial policy response were important factors behind the fall in private investment. Although an independent effect of "debt overhang" indicators on private investment could not be identified for most countries, this should certainly not be interpreted as meaning that the debt crisis—and its resolution—did not have a major impact on investment and growth. Obviously, such factors were of major importance, but they tended to operate indirectly through their impact on other variables—notably interest rates and the availability of credit to the private sector. In fact, other evidence indicates that the resolution of debt and debt-servicing diffi-

---

[61]Some of the available evidence is discussed in Appendix I, section on External Financing and the External Economic Environment.

[62]Increased use of foreign saving would generally raise GDP more than GNP because of the need to service the foreign borrowing; however, a sufficiently long time series for all eight countries is only available for GDP. The correlation between the average per capita growth rate and changes in net external financing as a share of GDP over two periods (1983–88 and 1989–93) was about 0.3 for the eight countries; similar results have been obtained for broader groups of developing countries.

[63]The panel regressions for a broader group of countries discussed in Section V suggest that, on average and after controlling for other influences including the terms of trade, about 40–50 percent of any increase in foreign saving goes to raise domestic consumption.

[64]The periods shown in the chart were chosen because they represent the times of largest changes in net external financing for many of the eight countries. In each case, the computed change is with respect to the average for the preceding five-year period. The correlation between changes in net external financing and changes in domestic investment for the eight countries is much higher (about 0.7 and 0.5, respectively, for the two periods) than the correlations with growth, but causation is likely to run in both directions.

Chart 17. Selected Developing Countries: Comparison of Changes in Investment and Net External Financing[1]

(In percent of GDP)

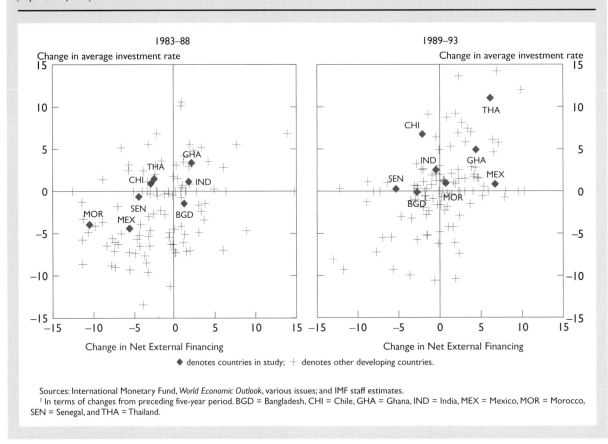

◆ denotes countries in study;   ＋ denotes other developing countries.

Sources: International Monetary Fund, *World Economic Outlook*, various issues; and IMF staff estimates.
[1] In terms of changes from preceding five-year period. BGD = Bangladesh, CHI = Chile, GHA = Ghana, IND = India, MEX = Mexico, MOR = Morocco, SEN = Senegal, and THA = Thailand.

culties typically raised investment. For example, the impact of Mexico's agreement with commercial bank creditors during 1989–90 appears to have been more important for its effects on the private sector's perceptions of creditworthiness and economic prospects than for its direct cash flow impact (equivalent to a total annual net saving on contractual interest payments of a little over ½ of 1 percent of GDP). Although it is difficult to disentangle the effects of the bank deal from policy measures, domestic real interest rates and Mexico's risk premiums did fall sharply soon after the announcement of the preliminary agreement in 1989 on the bank package (see Chart 14).[65]

Second, Bangladesh, Ghana, and Senegal experienced sizable increases in official external financing

at some point during their adjustment cycle, but with different outcomes for growth. In Ghana, the additional financing following the adoption of the Economic Recovery Program in 1983 appears to have had a major beneficial effect on the growth response to adjustment through several channels: (1) by alleviating a starvation of imported intermediate inputs essential for production, which appears to have been a factor behind the initial improvement in productivity; (2) by supporting a recovery in public investment; and (3) by improving confidence through the elimination of arrears and a modest rebuilding of reserves.[66] Increased official financing also helped improve the social and political acceptability of adjustment, including through the Program of Actions to Mitigate the Social Costs of Adjustment (PAM-

---

[65]See also the discussion in Loser and Kalter (1992), Section VII. In addition, Claessens, Oks, and van Wijnbergen (1994) found a positive effect on private investment in Mexico of a reduced variance in debt-service obligations following the bank deal.

[66]Growing arrears problems and a rundown in reserves forced a collapse in import volume during 1982–83 to barely half the level of three years earlier. The largest part of the external "financing" during 1980–82 consisted of a buildup in arrears. See Nowak and others (forthcoming).

Chart 18. Total Net External Financing[1]
(In percent of GDP)

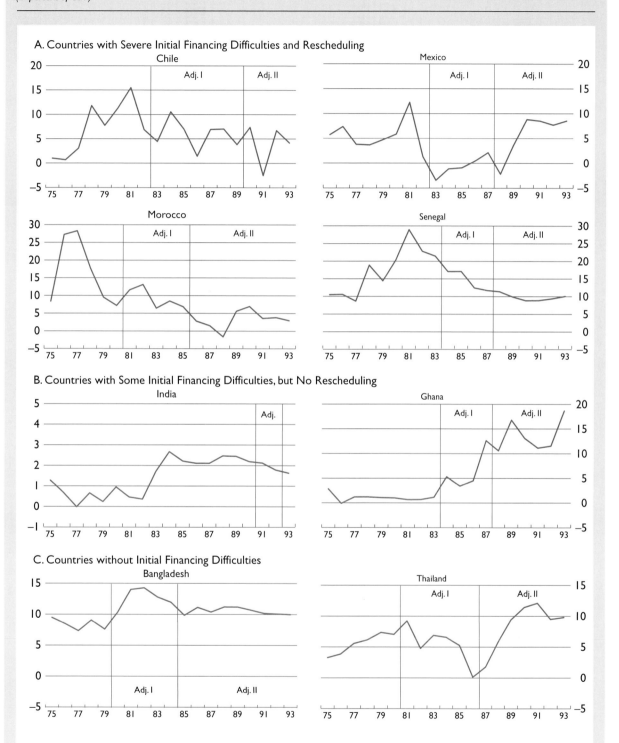

A. Countries with Severe Initial Financing Difficulties and Rescheduling

B. Countries with Some Initial Financing Difficulties, but No Rescheduling

C. Countries without Initial Financing Difficulties

Sources: International Monetary Fund, *World Economic Outlook*, various issues, and *International Financial Statistics*; and World Bank, *World Tables*.

[1] Net external financing equals the current account deficit plus the net increase in assets on portfolio and other investment account (including errors and omissions) plus the change in gross reserves. See Table 10.

Table 10. Periods of Sharpest Swings in Net External Financing[1]

(Annual averages in percent of GDP; at current prices)

		Net External Financing[2]							
			Of which						
		Private			Gross exceptional financing from IMF and World Bank[5]	Total Fixed Investment	National Saving	
	Total	Foreign direct investment	Other[3]	Net official[4]				Total	Public
Bangladesh									
1977–79	8.0	—	1.1	6.9	0.7	12.6	4.0	−2.5
1981–83	13.7	—	−1.3	15.0	1.4	13.4	4.3	−3.6
1991–93	10.1	0.1	0.4	9.6	0.6	12.5	10.4	0.1
Chile									
1979–81	11.5	0.9	11.1	−0.5	—	16.5	10.0	8.3
1985–87	5.1	2.4	−0.3	3.1	2.6	17.8	12.2	4.3
1990–92	3.9	1.3	1.2	1.4	—	22.3	24.6	6.5
Ghana									
1980–82	0.8	0.1	−0.7	1.4	0.1	4.8	4.3	−4.3
1983–85	3.3	—	1.8	1.5	2.1	6.7	6.6	−0.2
1989–91	13.7	0.3	0.6	12.7	3.5	15.2	12.2	5.4
India									
1988–90	2.4	0.1	1.4	0.9	—	23.2	22.6	1.5
1991–92	2.0	0.1	1.1	0.8	0.9	21.6	21.7	1.9
1993–94	1.2	0.3	0.3	0.6	—	20.0	20.3	…
Mexico									
1980–81	9.1	1.1	7.3	0.6	—	25.6	23.4	…
1983–85	−1.8	0.3	−2.9	0.8	0.5	18.2	25.3	…
1991–93	8.3	1.4	6.5	0.4	0.2	20.2	15.9	6.7
Morocco									
1976–78	24.5	0.4	20.7	3.4	0.8	25.8	16.1	−5.3
1983–85	7.2	0.3	−1.3	8.3	1.4	23.6	18.9	−4.6
1986–88	0.9	0.4	−4.0	4.5	0.8	20.6	22.5	−1.2
1989–91	5.4	1.0	2.8	1.6	0.6	23.0	22.2	0.6
Senegal									
1975–77	9.9	1.6	2.7	5.6	0.5	13.3	14.7	1.6
1980–82	24.0	2.2	13.2	8.6	2.9	14.0	−0.4	−3.4
1986–88	11.9	−0.7	3.3	9.3	2.6	12.3	5.8	1.2
Thailand									
1979–81	7.9	0.5	5.2	2.1	0.8	27.1	21.5	1.2
1985–87	2.4	0.5	1.5	0.4	0.4	26.9	26.0	2.4
1990–92	11.0	1.8	8.9	0.3	—	40.3	33.7	9.9

Sources: IMF staff estimates; and International Monetary Fund, *World Economic Outlook,* various issues.

[1]Based on three-year periods that show the largest swings in average net external financing as a share of GDP; two-year periods for Mexico (1980–81) and India (1991–92).

[2]Equals current account deficit plus the net increase in assets on portfolio and other investment account (including errors and omissions) plus change in gross official reserves. *World Economic Outlook* data do not identify separately private and official current transfers. For Bangladesh, Ghana, Senegal, and Thailand total current transfers are largely official and are excluded from the current account deficit for the purposes of calculating net external financing.

[3]Includes net portfolio investment (the data do not allow the separate identification of inward portfolio inflows) plus net external borrowing from banks.

[4]For Bangladesh, Ghana, Senegal, and Thailand includes total current transfers. Includes World Bank disbursements separately identified as exceptional financing.

[5]Equals IMF purchases (excluding reserve tranche) plus disbursements under the IMF's structural adjustment facility and enhanced structural adjustment facility plus World Bank disbursements under structural adjustment loans.

SCAD).[67] Equally important, however, was the fact that increased external financing was accompanied by a marked improvement in public saving.

In contrast, higher official financing to Bangladesh at the outset of the first adjustment period also supported higher public investment, but was accompanied by a deterioration in public saving. This constrained the availability of domestic counterpart funds for investment projects.[68] Evidence from Senegal during the early 1980s confirms that even massive inflows of external financing will not have a substantial impact on longer-term growth if the right policies are not put in place; inflows soared to over 20 percent of Senegal's GDP in the early 1980s and helped cushion consumption and investment against severe adverse terms of trade movements and drought-related supply shocks, but did not support lasting adjustment measures.

Third, several countries experienced substantial surges in private capital inflows at a later stage of the adjustment process: in Chile, Mexico, and Thailand these began in the late 1980s, and in India beginning in 1993. Availability of external financing was obviously not a constraint on growth during these episodes, but the inflows were associated with widely varying developments in saving and investment and hence in growth. Again, policies appear to be an important part of the explanation for the different outcomes. In Chile and Thailand, the inflows helped finance a large increase in private investment while national saving as a share of GDP rose either moderately (Chile) or substantially (Thailand). By contrast, the inflows to Mexico financed mainly higher consumption; investment also rose, but by much less than in the other two countries.

The influence of policies on these outcomes operated through several channels, including the effects of the inflows on bank balance sheets and household liquidity constraints and the effects of fiscal policy

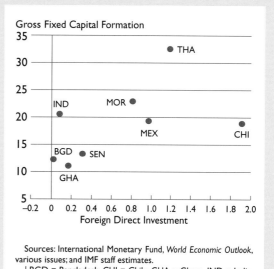

Chart 19. A Comparison of Foreign Direct Investment and Gross Fixed Capital Formation, 1982–93[1]

(Annual averages; in percent of GDP)

Sources: International Monetary Fund, *World Economic Outlook*, various issues; and IMF staff estimates.
[1] BGD = Bangladesh, CHI = Chile, GHA = Ghana, IND = India, MEX = Mexico, MOR = Morocco, SEN = Senegal, and THA = Thailand.

on aggregate demand and the real exchange rate.[69] In Chile, concerted efforts were made to discourage short-term inflows, including through the creation of some downside risk for the exchange rate and limiting the expansion in bank balance sheets. In Mexico, the capital inflows took place at a time of financial liberalization and contributed to a massive expansion of bank balance sheets. As indicated in Section V, the resulting easing of household liquidity constraints may have contributed to the decline in Mexico's private saving.

Chile, Mexico, and Thailand—but not India—started the period of capital inflows with strong fiscal positions, but only Thailand achieved a significant fiscal contraction in response to the inflows; in Chile, the fiscal position changed little, while in Mexico and India some fiscal relaxation occurred (although in Mexico the fiscal position remained in surplus). The more restrained fiscal stance in Thailand, by influencing the level and composition of aggregate demand, also affected the real exchange rate path and probably helped to avoid a real appreciation. But other factors, including an overall policy

---

[67]PAMSCAD represented a comprehensive attempt at addressing social strains created by macroeconomic adjustment over the period 1988–89. It included financing of infrastructure rehabilitation, public works projects, and addressing the basic needs of the poor. PAMSCAD was to be fully funded by foreign aid. However, because of slow disbursements and implementation difficulties less than one fifth of the pledged donor assistance materialized by mid-1992. Mainly because of this financing shortfall, but also as a result of inadequate cost management and targeting, the goals of PAMSCAD were less than fully realized. See Nowak and others (forthcoming) and Roe and Schneider (1992).

[68]In Bangladesh, persistent shortfalls from program targets for external financing occurred in the second adjustment period, but appear to have reflected difficulties in implementing the public investment program rather than a shortage of potential external financing.

---

[69]The causes and consequences of capital inflows into Chile, Mexico, and Thailand are discussed in more depth in Schadler, Carkovic, Bennett, and Kahn (1993). See also Khan and Reinhart (1995).

framework that is conducive to foreign direct investment (FDI), have also been important. Such capital flows have been viewed as especially beneficial to growth because, in addition to their direct contributions to financing domestic investment, they are an important vehicle for the transfer of technology. Cross-country estimates by Borensztein and others (1995) suggest that there are significant crowding-in effects (a net inflow of FDI is associated with an increase in total investment at least one and a half times as large) and that there is a strong complementarity between FDI and human capital (FDI is more likely to be productive when human capital endowments exceed a minimum threshold level). Such inflows have been especially important in Chile and

Thailand over the last decade (Chart 19); indeed, direct investment into Thailand was probably much larger than suggested by available statistics.[70]

---

[70]Data on the nature of the inflows vary in quality and disaggregation and definitions are not uniform across countries. Recorded FDI was, on average, in the range of 1½ percent to 2 percent of GDP in Chile, Mexico, and Thailand during the recent periods of peak capital inflows. However, Thailand's data tend to understate substantially the share of FDI, much of which appears to be recorded as inflows into the banking system. See also Bercuson and Koenig (1993). FDI also rose to these levels in Morocco during 1991–93, in part reflecting foreign acquisitions of privatized assets. The capital inflows to India have been dominated by portfolio equity capital (see Chopra and others (1995)).

VIII Structural Reforms

Structural reforms aimed at increasing the role of the market and the private sector can enhance growth by improving the efficiency of resource allocation and by expanding the productive capacity of the economy. While this is a widely accepted notion, the empirical basis for making judgments on the effects of particular reforms on growth is often not well established. The difficulty of deriving simple quantitative measures to summarize the complex nature of structural reforms makes it hard to identify statistically robust relationships.[71] Moreover, supply shocks and other exogenous factors can greatly affect measured productivity changes in the short term. Bearing in mind these constraints, two different approaches are used here to illustrate the links between structural reforms and output and productivity growth. First, evidence from the eight countries on the potential impact of various structural policies on productivity growth suggests that certain critical clusters of reforms appear to enhance efficiency gains. Although this information, by its nature, is difficult to compare across countries, some important common messages emerge; more detailed lessons for individual countries are summarized in Box 5. Second, an attempt is made to identify how closely trade and financial sector reforms in particular countries appear to have followed what are generally regarded as "best practices," deemed most likely to yield an early response of investment and productivity. Fiscal, administrative, and public enterprise reform are discussed in more detail in the companion study.[72]

Reforms and Productivity

What are the main messages from the eight countries with regard to reforms and productivity? To set the stage for the discussion, Table 11 presents a ranking of the countries by the severity of structural distortions in the 1970s. Using a categorization by Agarwala (1983) covering five key structural areas,

it is possible to rank the countries as follows: Mexico and Thailand began with the fewest structural distortions, with Chile and Morocco in an intermediate category, whereas distortions were greatest in Bangladesh, Ghana, India, and Senegal.[73]

An examination of overall productivity (or TFP) trends in each country, drawing upon the information presented in Section II, suggests that countries that made the most progress in removing structural distortions, or where structural distortions were not large to begin with, were typically among the ones with more rapid growth in measured productivity (Chart 20). Chile made the most progress in implementing far-reaching structural reforms that served to increase substantially the role of the private sector in the economy. Thailand's starting position of a relatively undistorted incentive structure and its long-standing policy stance of favoring the private sector also appear to have been associated with sustained productivity gains, despite the relatively slow pace of further structural reform. Other countries that experienced considerable initial productivity gains were those that began with severe structural distortions. For example, Ghana's policies to decontrol prices and liberalize the exchange and trade regimes early in the adjustment process were followed by substantial productivity gains during the 1980s; to some extent, however, these may have reflected one-time gains stemming from the reversal of previous disastrous policies. Appreciable increases in TFP also took place in Bangladesh and India, where considerable, if uneven, progress was made in correcting distortions in key sectors. At the opposite end of the scale, Senegal's slow and faltering progress in structural reforms appears to have been associated with slow growth in TFP during the adjustment period.

---

[71]Available evidence is discussed in Appendices I and II.

[72]Mackenzie and others (forthcoming).

[73]Such classifications involve a considerable measure of judgment. The rankings do not cover less quantifiable factors such as regulatory complexities, which were the most severe in Bangladesh and India. Morocco was not included in the Agarwala sample, but available information suggests that it falls into the category of moderate initial distortions.

Box 5. How Could Structural Reforms Have Been More Growth Enhancing?

With the benefit of hindsight, a different pace or composition of reforms might have been more growth enhancing in the eight countries. Abstracting from the fact that programs have to be designed to take into account administrative and political constraints, the following are the main lessons that emerge from the case studies.

Bangladesh

• Slow progress in public enterprise reform hampered financial sector development (and hence investment) by contributing to weaknesses in bank portfolios and also slowed the progress of trade reforms because of pressures to protect weak public enterprises.

• More extensive technical preparation at an early stage, aimed at improving public enterprise accounts, would have helped to identify the scope of the needed reforms.

• Financial sector reforms did not emphasize the strengthening of prudential regulations and bank supervision sufficiently early.

Chile

• Financial sector reforms included the early privatization of banks and a gradual liberalization of interest rates. However, weak bank supervision and a high concentration of ownership allowed excessive risk-taking in domestic and foreign currency operations. Rapid credit expansion at a time of high real interest rates should have been taken as a signal of bank portfolio problems, indicating the need for early corrective action to strengthen supervision and tighten prudential requirements.

Ghana

• Price reforms in agriculture would have yielded a faster supply response if they had been complemented by an early deregulation of cocoa marketing and increased emphasis on the provision of agricultural extension services.

• Insufficient attention to weaknesses in the banking system and continued financial repression discouraged financial savings.

• Faster progress in reducing the public sector's role in key sectors of the economy (for example, gold production and cocoa exporting) would have stimulated greater private sector activity and yielded greater productivity gains.

India

• An earlier start and more rapid progress in reforming the tax system and earlier action to remove quantitative restrictions on consumer imports, would have eased the trade-off between tariff reform and fiscal consolidation.

• More progress in restructuring or closing "sick" companies (in the public and private sectors) would have eased pressure on the financial system and the budget, as well as enhancing productivity gains.

• A broadening of the reforms to cover the agricultural sector, where pricing distortions are still considerable, would have offered scope for considerable productivity gains.

• Adjustment programs have been largely concentrated at the level of the central government. The competition for investment has spurred reforms in some states, but in others the reform process has barely begun and distortions and inefficiencies remain.

• Faster progress to put in place a supporting framework governing private investment in areas previously reserved for the public sector (for example, power and telecommunications) would have reduced delays in the private investment response and eased interim supply bottlenecks.

Mexico

• Extensive trade liberalization since 1985 yielded a strong export response. However, a marked real exchange rate appreciation after 1987 eroded the competitiveness of import-competing sectors.

• Important progress was made in the privatization of public enterprises and increased private sector participation in some infrastructural sectors. Nevertheless, inefficiencies in infrastructure in railroads and telecommunications, together with limited progress in agricultural sector reform, continued to constrain growth. A number of important reforms have been introduced into these latter areas in the last several years, but may be too recent to have yet had a major impact on productivity.

• Financial sector reforms introduced since 1989 succeeded in reversing earlier disintermediation. Nevertheless, insufficient progress in evaluating credit risk at a time of rapid expansion in bank balance sheets increased the incidence of nonperforming bank loans. Limited competition in the banking system, partly on account of restricted entry of foreign banks, remained a constraining factor on the growth of small and medium-sized enterprises.

Morocco

• Trade reforms were supported by an initially flexible exchange rate policy; reforms of the domestic tax system; removal of price controls, including on producer prices; and liberalization of marketing arrangements. However, even after the reforms the level and dispersion of tariffs remained quite high, a complex set of investment incentives and exemptions distorted resource allocation signals, and price controls remained.

• Faster progress in liberalizing interest rates and removing the large-scale pre-emption of financial resources by the public sector would have speeded the development of a more efficient and competitive financial sector.

• Substantive reform of the large public enterprise sector has occurred only in the last several years. An

Box 5 *(concluded)*

earlier start, together with a transparent regulatory framework for private sector activity in areas previously reserved for the public sector, would have yielded earlier efficiency gains and a faster response by domestic and foreign investors.
• The outdated commercial codes and lack of a comprehensive legal reference system also deterred the investment response.

Senegal
• Removal of distortions in the pricing of major cash crops would have facilitated a faster supply response to other agricultural reforms.
• Slow progress with public enterprise, industrial policy, and labor market reform impeded private sector development.

• Insufficient fiscal reform and an overvalued exchange rate resulted in almost full reversal of trade reforms.

Thailand
• Earlier implementation of domestic tax reform would have permitted a more rapid pace of tariff reforms.
• Delays in removing interest rate controls and in introducing greater competition in the banking system contributed, until recently, to the wide spread between deposit and lending rates.
• Nevertheless, the relatively low level of structural distortions meant that the generally modest pace of structural reforms was not a major impediment to growth.

Productivity developments in Mexico and Morocco do not appear to be explained solely by the extent of structural distortions. Such distortions were not only moderate to begin with, but both countries made major progress in several key areas, such as domestic and trade taxation, price liberalization, and financial sector reform. For Morocco, in addition to the influence of adverse supply shocks, the relatively

low TFP growth has been attributed to the low rate of accumulation of human capital, as evidenced by the limited improvements in basic education and training, delays in financial sector reforms, and the continued dominance of the public sector in key areas. As for Mexico, although the reasons for the low TFP growth are not fully understood, and may partly reflect the inherent limitations (discussed in

Table 11. Severity of Structural Distortions in the 1970s

	Effective Rate of Protection (ERP) of Manufacturing[1]	Financial Repression[2]	Taxation of Agriculture[3]	Infrastructure Pricing Distortions[4]	Labor Market Distortions[5]
Bangladesh	High	High	Moderate	High	High
Chile	Low	High	Low	High	High
Ghana	High	High	High	High	Moderate
India	High	Moderate	Moderate	High	High
Mexico	Low	High	Low	Moderate	Moderate
Senegal	Moderate	Moderate	High	High	High
Thailand	Moderate	Low	Low	High	Low

Sources: Agarwala (1983) and IMF staff estimates.

[1]High is when ERP is greater than 80 percent; low is when ERP is less than 40 percent; and moderate otherwise.

[2]High is when real interest rates are less than −5 percent; low is when real rates are positive; and moderate otherwise.

[3]High is when the implicit taxation (or protection) rate is greater than 30 percent; low when it is less than 10 percent; and moderate otherwise.

[4]Proxied by distortions in pricing in the power sector. High is when rate of return on asset base in power utilities is less than 4 percent; low when rate of return is greater than 8 percent; and moderate otherwise. However, India was reclassified as "high" (rather than moderate) because other pricing distortions were large.

[5]High is when real wage growth is considerably faster than productivity growth and there is marked intervention in labor market or the presence of powerful labor unions or both; low when neither is true; moderate when both are present in weak form. India and Senegal were reclassified as "high" rather than "moderate" because of the presence of significant labor market rigidities.

Chart 20. Export Market Shares and Real Effective Exchange Rates[1]

(In percentage points)

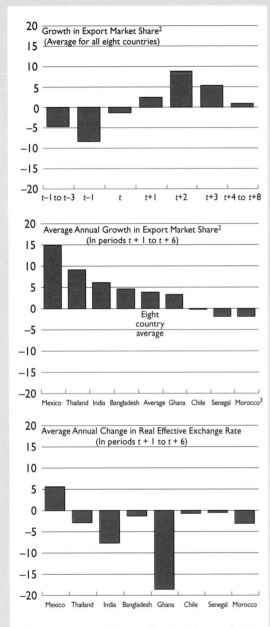

Sources: International Monetary Fund, *World Economic Outlook*, various issues, Information Notice System, *International Financial Statistics*; and IMF staff estimates.

[1] *t* is the initial year of reform in each country; for India, data are only available through *t* + 3.

[2] Growth in export market share is defined as the growth in each country's export volume less the growth in partner countries' non-oil import volumes. For Mexico, non-oil export volumes are used.

[3] Average for (*t* + 1) to (*t* + 5) to exclude temporary fall in phosphate exports in 1989 (*t* + 6) owing to a trade dispute.

Section II) of the residual TFP measure, the World Bank has identified weaknesses in the financial system, especially the high cost of credit to small and medium private enterprises, as well as lagging reforms in the agricultural sector as important impediments to more rapid efficiency gains (see World Bank (1994b)). There are, however, signs that, prior to the recent crisis earlier structural initiatives were beginning to yield productivity gains in the manufacturing sector.[74]

Specific messages about the links between structural reforms and growth that emerge from the eight countries are as follows.

• The extent of the public enterprise sector and the pace of its reform appear to have been important in influencing productivity in a number of countries. For example, in India,[75] industry-specific studies suggest that rates of return on investment in public manufacturing enterprises were very low (and much lower than the returns to public investment in infrastructure) and showed little improvement through most of the period under review. In contrast, estimated rates of return on investment in private manufacturing were always substantially higher and appear to have risen over time, perhaps in response to the limited liberalization of industrial, trade, financial, and tax policies that began in the 1980s. These findings suggest that there is a large potential payoff, in terms of efficiency gains, from more aggressive public enterprise reform, including privatization. In a number of countries, incomplete public enterprise reforms have also resulted in continuing fiscal problems and have proven to be an obstacle to more substantial trade reforms (Bangladesh, India, and Senegal), and deeper progress with financial sector reforms (Bangladesh and Ghana).

• Price decontrol and reduction of state intervention in domestic marketing are important complements to trade and exchange market reforms. They are also more likely to elicit a strong supply response when accompanied by concerted efforts to improve physical and institutional infrastructural support. Slow progress in these areas appears to have been detrimental to efficiency gains in key productive sectors in Ghana, Morocco, and Senegal.

• Extensive industrial regulation and heavy government intervention in investment choices have deterred productivity growth in some countries. The starkest example is India, where capital-intensive industries favored by trade and regulatory barriers and given preferential access to credit generally experienced lower TFP growth than other sectors.

---

[74]Average output per worker in Mexican manufacturing rose at an annual average rate of 6 percent during the period 1988–94.

[75]See Chopra and others (1995).

• A sustained increase in private sector participation in areas previously reserved for the public sector requires the early installation of an appropriate institutional and regulatory framework aimed at signaling transparency and predictability in the direction of policy changes. Delays in the establishment of such a framework acted as a drag on private investment in India and Mexico.

The focus of the rest of this section is on a closer examination of reforms of the trade and financial systems.

Trade Reforms

The benefits of trade reform for growth can be ascribed to more efficient resource allocation following comparative advantage, the exploitation of scale economies, as well as to the possibility that a more open trade system encourages innovation and allows knowledge to more easily cross national borders.[76] Cross-country studies of trade reforms have typically identified a number of "best practices." Reforms are generally more successful in generating a rapid supply response and are less likely to be reversed when (1) they begin with a substantial initial effort; (2) they involve rapid dismantling of quantitative restrictions (QRs); (3) the exchange rate provides signals for exports and import-competing sectors that are consistent with medium-term external sustainability; and (4) they are accompanied, where necessary, by a liberalization of domestic markets and price controls. Each of these elements is important not only to furnish appropriate price incentives but also to increase confidence in the permanence of the reforms. Efficient adjustment in the allocation of resources will be impeded, and the dynamic growth effects dampened, if trade reforms are perceived to be short-lived.

How Closely Were Best Practices Followed?

Table 12 presents some indicators of trade distortions before and after the reforms, and Table 13 indicates how closely the reforms followed the best practices.[77] Chile and Ghana made the most progress. In these two countries, bold trade reforms were accompanied by large initial depreciations of the real effective exchange rate and substantial tax

reforms.[78] Significant trade liberalization was also achieved in Mexico and Morocco. In Mexico, reforms initiated in 1985 were accompanied by a real effective exchange rate depreciation during the first two years of reform; subsequently, the real exchange rate appreciated when the nominal exchange rate was pegged in order to anchor inflation expectations. In Morocco, trade liberalization was supported by major reforms of the tax system, liberalization of domestic trade, some reductions in price controls, and a significant real exchange rate depreciation during most of the 1980s.[79]

Bangladesh and India followed best practices in some respects, but with important exceptions: despite some liberalization and simplification, quantitative restrictions remain pervasive and the trade systems are still quite restrictive. In both countries, reductions in high average tariff rates involved difficult trade-offs with the goal of fiscal consolidation.

Finally, neither Senegal nor Thailand followed best practices in their reforms. Many of Senegal's trade reforms of the mid-1980s were reversed after only three years because of fiscal problems. Thailand also implemented only moderate reforms, and some of the initial tariff reductions were temporarily reversed because of conflicts with tax revenue goals.

Supply Responses

The performance of exports following trade reforms warrants special attention because it is the area where the supply response can be most readily identified and because such reforms are unlikely to be sustained if they do not result in faster export growth.[80] However, the potential benefits of trade reform for growth are obviously not limited to the export sector.

On average, the export response (measured by an unweighted average of the growth in export market shares of each country) appears to be strongly positive and is typically realized within one to two years after the initiation of trade reforms (Chart 20). The variation in the supply response among countries serves to highlight the crucial linkages between trade reforms and other aspects of structural and macroeconomic policies. In particular, the following two aspects appear to be especially important:

---

[76]A detailed analysis of the impact of trade reforms in IMF-supported programs is contained in Kirmani and others, Vol. II (1994).

[77]An outline of the principal measures taken in each country is given in Appendix V, Table 20.

[78]These tax reforms typically included a broadening of the base of domestic sales taxation by eliminating exemptions and preferential rates and/or through the introduction of a value-added tax; see Mackenzie and others (forthcoming).

[79]See Nsouli and others (1995).

[80]Changes in export performance as indicated by the growth in export market shares cannot be attributed exclusively to the reforms unless it is assumed that market shares would have remained unchanged otherwise, which is unlikely to be the case.

Table 12. Indicators of Trade Reform
(In percent unless otherwise indicated)

	Prereform	Year of Reform	Post-Reform
Bangladesh	*1980*	*1989*	*1993*
Average nominal tariff (unweighted)	...	94	50
Dispersion (standard deviation)	...	59	32
Import-weighted average tariff	...	17	43
Share of imports covered by QRs[1]	high	40	10
Number of tariff bands	24	11	...
Range of tariffs (high/low)	400/...	509/3	100/7.5
Real effective exchange rate[2]	1	−1	−1
Parallel market exchange premium	112	200	—
Total trade/GDP	23	23	25
Chile	*1970*	*1974*	*1992*
Average nominal tariff (unweighted)	105	35	11
Dispersion (standard deviation)	...	—	—
Import-weighted average tariff	>35	16	<10
Share of imports covered by QRs[1]	high	—	—
Number of tariff bands	many	1	1
Range of tariffs	750/0	35/35	11/11
Effective export taxes	...	—	—
Real effective exchange rate[2]	12	−33	3
Parallel market exchange premium	6	9	—
Total trade/GDP	...	37	47
Ghana	*1980*	*1983*	*1992*
Average nominal tariff (unweighted)	30	30	17
Import-weighted average tariff	12	17	7
Share of imports covered by QRs[3]	100	100	2
Number of tariff bands	3	3	4
Range of tariffs	50/10	30/10	25/0
Effective export taxes	27	31	5
Real effective exchange rate[2]	59	−41	−12
Parallel market exchange premium	304	223	<10
Total trade/GDP	8	14	35
India	*1985*	*1991*	*1993*
Average nominal tariff (unweighted)	100	128	71
Dispersion (standard deviation)	...	41	30
Import-weighted average tariff	55	87	47
Share of imports covered by QRs[4]	...	93	<50
Number of tariff bands	13	...	...
Range of tariffs (high/low)	...	400/0	85/0
Real effective exchange rate[2]	2	−13	2
Parallel market exchange premium	14	16	12
Total trade/GDP	12	15	16
Mexico	*1980*	*1985*	*1992*
Average nominal tariff[5]	23	24	13
Import-weighted average tariff	16	9	5
Share of imports covered by QRs[1]	64	92	<10
Number of tariff bands	16	11	5
Range of tariffs (high/low)	...	100/0	20/0
Effective export taxes	38	—	—
Real effective exchange rate[2]	−1	−12	7
Parallel market exchange premium	3	25	—
Total trade/GDP	17	19	23
Morocco	*1980*	*1983*	*1992*
Average nominal tariff (unweighted)	47	...	36
Import-weighted average tariff	24	20	18
Share of imports covered by QRs[1]	high	76	9
Number of tariff bands	...	26	9
Range of tariffs	...	400/0	35/0

Table 12 *(concluded)*

	Prereform	Year of Reform	Post-Reform
Effective export taxes	2	2	1
Real effective exchange rate[2]	–4	–6	1
Parallel market exchange premium	—	9	10
Total trade/GDP	37	43	37
Senegal	*1970*	*1974*	*1992*
Average nominal tariff (unweighted)	...	98	90
Import-weighted average tariff	...	23	30
Share of imports covered by QRs[1]	high	high	...
Number of tariff bands	...	...	...
Range of tariffs (high/low)	...	190/0	128/0
Effective export taxes	...	...	
Real effective exchange rate[2]	–4	–1	–2
Parallel market exchange premium	—	—	—
Total trade/GDP	55	36	33
Thailand	*1980*	*1984*	*1992*
Average nominal tariff (unweighted)	31	34	30
Import-weighted average tariff	11	13	9
Dispersion (coefficient of variation)	30	27	25
Share of imports covered by QRs[1]	<5	<5	<5
Number of tariff bands	...	...	39
Range of tariffs (high/low)	...	60/0	200/0
Effective export taxes	3	1	—
Real effective exchange rate[2]	5	–8	–1
Parallel market exchange premium	—	—	—
Total trade/GDP	44	40	62

Source: IMF staff estimates.

[1] As a percentage of tariff lines.

[2] Forward-looking three-year average, except for the post-reform period.

[3] Number of goods or categories.

[4] As a percentage of domestic production.

[5] As a percentage of tradable goods production

• The supply response depends on the strength of supporting sectoral reforms. The shift from massively distorted systems and the concurrent simplification of complex and restrictive exchange regimes appears to have been associated with a pickup in export growth in Bangladesh, Ghana, and India. However, the experience of these three countries suggests that greater efficiency gains would have been forthcoming if certain critical supporting sectoral-level reforms had accompanied the trade and exchange reforms. As an illustration, Box 6 outlines some factors that appear to have impeded the supply response in Ghana. In Bangladesh and India, trade liberalization appears to have facilitated the process of reallocating resources in accordance with comparative advantage—in part, because of the predominance of informal, and highly flexible, labor markets in many sectors. However, several factors appear to have reduced some of the immediate productivity gains from the reforms: (1) pressures to protect weak public enterprises, which often led to continued bank lending; (2) especially in India, the existence of barriers to the exit of resources from noncompetitive sectors, including de jure or de facto restrictions on laying off workers in the formal sector; and (3) delayed implementation of legal and institutional reform to accompany broader industrial deregulation.

• Real effective exchange rate movements are also important. For example, the low average growth of export market shares in Chile during the early years following trade reform appears to be due, in part, to the appreciation of the real effective exchange rate, reflecting the trade-off faced by the Chilean authorities between the goals of disinflation and competitiveness in their exchange-rate-based stabilization program of 1978–82. Export growth accelerated markedly during the 1980s as competitiveness was restored. Trade liberalization in Mexico was followed by a strong response of manufactured (but not agricultural) exports, especially in the first two post-reform years, but the post-1987 real effective exchange rate appreciation was also associated

Table 13. Key Characteristics of Trade Reforms and Export Response

A. Key Characteristics of Trade Reforms

Country (Initial year of reforms)	Bold Start	Early Reduction of QRs	Stable Macroeconomic Environment	Supporting Domestic Tax Reforms	Reversal of Reforms	Supportive Exchange Rate Policy
Bangladesh (1985)	No	No	Yes	Yes	No	No
Chile (1974)	Yes	Yes	No	Yes	No	Yes
Ghana (1983)	Yes	Yes	Partial	Yes	Partial	Yes
India (1991)	Yes	Partial	Yes	Yes	No	Yes
Mexico (1985)	Yes	Yes	No	Yes	No	Initially: Yes Later: No
Morocco (1983)	Yes	Yes	Yes	Yes	No	Yes
Senegal (1986)	No	Yes	No	No	Yes	No
Thailand (1984)	No	No significant QRs	Yes	Partial	Partial	Yes

B. Export Response

Country (Initial year of reforms)	Average of Three Years Prior to Reforms	Year Prior to Reforms (In percent)	Initial Year of Reforms (t)	Post-Reforms Year t + 1	Year t + 2	Year t + 3
Bangladesh (1985)						
Export volume growth	1	−2	6	25	15	−5
Growth in export market share[1]	−8	−16	1	19	6	−11
Chile (1974)						
Export volume growth	—	5	31	−9	21	2
Growth in export market share[1]	−12	−9	18	−4	11	−6
Ghana (1983)						
Export volume growth	−1	12	−28	4	19	11
Growth in export market share[1]	−4	10	−32	−5	16	6
India (1991)						
Export volume growth	12	7	−1	1	15	22
Growth in export market share[1]	3	1	−4	−4	9	11
Mexico (1985)						
Export volume growth[2]	13	19	−7	41	33	12
Growth in export market share[1]	−2	−6	−14	31	25	7
Morocco (1983)						
Export volume growth	2	1	10	5	2	7
Growth in export market share[1]	−4	−4	8	−2	−13	1
Senegal (1986)						
Export volume growth	−6	−19	13	−10	5	22
Growth in export market share[1]	−11	−24	7	−18	−2	13
Thailand (1984)						
Export volume growth	1	−9	17	−6	21	23
Growth in export market share[1]	−4	−14	3	−8	15	8

Sources: IMF staff estimates; and International Monetary Fund, *World Economic Outlook*, various issues.

[1]Defined as the difference between partner countries' non-oil import volume growth less each countries' export volume growth.

[2]Non-oil export volume.

Box 6. Ghana: Constraints to a Stronger Supply Response

Prior to 1983, Ghana had a highly distorted domestic price system—particularly discriminating against agriculture[1]—a restrictive trade and exchange regime with a massively overvalued exchange rate, a monopolistic market structure dominated by state-owned enterprises, and a complex and rigid legal and regulatory framework.

Trade reforms were initiated early in the adjustment process; overall, they were implemented consistently and at a rapid pace, despite some partial reversal (see Table 12). They were complemented by an initial major exchange rate realignment, followed by more gradual exchange reform that served to eliminate exchange rate overvaluation by 1986. However, the supply response was weaker and slower to materialize than expected, despite progress in price decontrol early in the adjustment process. The main reason appears to be that supporting sectoral-level measures were delayed, inhibiting private sector initiative and hindering the efficient reallocation of resources.

First, agriculture, the largest sector, continued to suffer from price discrimination, despite evidence of a high price elasticity of agricultural supply, with enormous costs in terms of forgone agricultural income.[2] As a result, growth in agriculture—which was also hampered by bottlenecks in infrastructure and lack of extension services in rural areas—picked up only marginally, and at 2.7 percent on average during the 1980s, fell far short of the developing country average of about 4 percent. Second, privatization was delayed,[3] in effect maintaining the dominant position of the state-owned enterprises that because of overstaffing, extensive involvement in noncommercial operations, and monopoly power were less sensitive to improved incentives.[4] Third, labor market rigidities persisted, particularly in the public sector, characterized by wage setting disconnected from productivity increases, unduly generous nonwage benefits, and restrictions on labor mobility. Fourth, financial sector reform did not get off the ground for several years after the adjustment program was launched. Finally, foreign investment remained modest, limiting the ability of the private sector to take full advantage of exchange and trade liberalization.

[1]Ghana had the highest direct and indirect taxes on agriculture during 1960–84 among 18 developing countries examined by Krueger, Schiff and Valdes (1991).
[2]The World Bank (1993a) estimated that annual agricultural growth rates during 1980–93 could have been raised by 1½–2 percentage points, if real farm prices had been 30 percent higher.

[3]Divestment of government ownership began only in 1994, when the Government's controlling stake in seven companies listed on the Ghana Stock Exchange, including the Ashanti Gold Mines, was sold to foreign investors.
[4]For example, the Cocoa Board had a monopoly position in the marketing and export of cocoa (the biggest export earner) and the Ghana National Petroleum Corporation monopolized the importation and distribution of oil products.

---

with a substantial loss in competitiveness in import-competing sectors. Finally, Senegal's poor performance in exports and overall productivity appears to be associated with both the lack of supporting structural reforms and an overvalued exchange rate.

Financial Sector Reforms

The link between financial sector reforms and growth works primarily through establishing more efficient channels of intermediation between financial saving and investment.[81] Best practices most likely to yield efficiency gains from financial sector reforms include (1) achieving and maintaining macroeconomic stability; (2) elimination of severe financial repression (that is, of significantly negative real interest rates) at an early stage of the reforms; (3) effective prudential regulation and supervision so that the reforms do not weaken bank balance sheets; and (4) where appropriate, supporting fiscal consolidation and reforms of the public enterprise sector. It is necessary to eliminate financial repression and keep real deposit rates positive to attract funds away from the informal toward the official sector where the real cost of borrowing tends to be lower and resource allocation more efficient. However, interest rate liberalization may be accompanied by substantial upward pressure on real lending (and deposit) rates if large public sector borrowing requirements are not reduced. In addition, excessive lending to financially weak public enterprises is frequently a major threat to bank portfolios.

Key elements of financial sector reforms in each country are presented in Appendix V, Table 21. Table 14 presents some indicators of conditions prior

[81]The link between more developed financial intermediation and growth has also been attributed to the idea that the former promotes innovative activity. King and Levine (1993) present cross-country evidence that higher levels of financial development are robustly correlated with higher rates of growth, capital formation, and efficiency improvements. The discussion in this section focuses on banking system reforms. Other financial sector reforms, such as the development of bond and equity capital markets, also help to improve the efficiency of financial intermediation. Atje and Jovanovic (1993) find evidence that the development of stock markets has a significant effect on growth.

Table 14. Indicators of Financial Sector Reforms
(In percent unless otherwise indicated)

	Prereform	Year of Reform	Post-Reform
Bangladesh	*1980*	*1988*	*1993*
Real deposit interest rates[1]	−6	1	2
Real lending interest rates[1]	−1	7	11
Spread between nominal lending and deposit rates	7	6	9
Ratio of broad money to GDP	16	29	33
Private sector's share of total credit	35	69	66
Private investment/GDP[2]	8	6	5
Chile[3]	*1974*	*1981*	*1993*
Real deposit interest rates[1]	...	23	3
Real lending interest rates[1]	...	33	9
Spread between nominal lending and deposit rates	...	11	6
Ratio of broad money to GDP	14	27	38
Private sector's share of total credit	22	104	80
Private investment/GDP[2]	...	14	20
Ghana	*1980*	*1988*	*1993*
Real deposit interest rates[1]	−23	−11	−4
Real lending interest rates[1]	−18	−5	4
Spread between nominal lending and deposit rates	6	7	10
Ratio of broad money to GDP	19	18	19
Private sector's share of total credit	10	17	24
Private investment/GDP[2]	3	7	4
India	*1980*	*1991*	*1993*
Real deposit interest rates[1]	−3	6	6
Real lending interest rates[1]	2	9	13
Spread between nominal lending and deposit rates	5	4	8
Ratio of broad money to GDP	39	48	48
Private sector's share of total credit	58	51	51
Private investment/GDP[2]	9	12	...
Mexico	*1980*	*1988*	*1993*
Real deposit interest rates[1]	−24	−16	8
Real lending interest rates[1]	−19	...	...
Spread between nominal lending and deposit rates	7	...	...
Ratio of broad money to GDP	29	11	31
Private sector's share of total credit	51	37	99
Private investment/GDP[2]	14	14	16
Morocco	*1980*	*1985*	*1993*
Real deposit interest rates[1]	−9	−	5
Real lending interest rates[1]	−7	−	6
Spread between nominal lending and deposit rates	2	−	1
Ratio of broad money to GDP	42	46	63
Private sector's share of total credit	38	35	45
Private investment/GDP[2]	18	17	20
Senegal	*1980*	*1988*	*1993*
Real deposit interest rates[1]	−5	3	8
Real lending interest rates[1]	3	11	17
Spread between nominal lending and deposit rates	8	8	9
Ratio of broad money to GDP	28	23	21
Private sector's share of total credit	55	49	69
Private investment/GDP[2]	9	9	10

Table 14 *(concluded)*

	Prereform	Year of Reform	Post-Reform
Thailand	*1981*	*1989*	*1993*
Real deposit interest rates[1]	4	3	4
Real lending interest rates[1]	10	8	7
Spread between nominal lending and deposit rates	7	6	3
Ratio of broad money to GDP	39	65	79
Private sector's share of total credit	72	93	105
Private investment/GDP[2]	19	22	32

Source: International Monetary Fund, *International Financial Statistics.*

[1]Ex-post real rates calculated using current period inflation of the GDP deflator, except for Mexico in 1980 where consumer price index inflation is used.

[2]Forward-looking three-year averages, except for 1993.

[3]In Chile, financial sector reforms were initiated in 1974; the reform process was deepened in 1981.

to and after the initiation of reforms.[82] Prior to the reforms, financial sectors can be characterized as being severely repressed in Bangladesh, Chile, Ghana, and Mexico; moderately repressed in Morocco and Senegal; and/or as having substantial government intervention in credit allocation in Bangladesh, Chile, India, and Mexico.[83]

How Closely Were Best Practices Followed?

Financial sector reforms went farthest and fastest in Chile where rapid progress was made in liberalizing interest rates, eliminating quantitative credit controls, and significantly restructuring the banking system. In many respects, Mexico can also be classified as having undertaken major reforms, although at a much later stage, with interest rates not decontrolled until the late 1980s and the banking system denationalized in 1991. Ghana, Morocco, and Senegal implemented more moderate financial sector reforms, which nevertheless reduced substantially the

degree of government intervention in this sector, whereas Bangladesh and India undertook only limited banking sector reforms.[84]

The main messages that emerge from the eight countries' experience with financial sector reforms follow.

• It is critically important to strengthen bank supervision and regulation along with financial liberalization. The case of Chile is especially instructive. While many elements of the reform process that began in the mid-1970s were implemented according to best practices, the initial results illustrate the risks of implementing reforms without strong and effective bank supervision and the potential serious macroeconomic consequence of weak bank balance sheets.[85] A significant part of the very rapid private sector credit growth took place to refinance a growing volume of nonperforming loans and ultimately resulted in a serious banking crisis in the early 1980s that greatly exacerbated the ensuing recession. The excessive lending took place at a time when ex-ante real interest rates appeared to be extremely high, which complicated judgments on the tightness of monetary policy. The principal cause of the problems appears to have been the poor design and implementation of prudential regulations in the early stages of the reform, when there was extensive deregulation of commercial banking in the context of an oligopolistic banking structure dominated by a few industrial companies. Subsequent reforms strengthened supervision and regulation and at-

---

[82]The efficacy of financial sector reforms in mobilizing financial saving and improving the efficiency with which resources are intermediated is difficult to measure directly. Typical summary indicators include the size of the financial system measured by the ratio of broad money to GDP, the private sector's share of total credit as a measure of asset distribution, and the spread between deposit and lending rates. King and Levine (1992 and 1993) find a positive association between the allocation of credit to the private sector and the rate of investment and productivity growth.

[83]Financial repression here refers to cases where real interest rates were significantly negative over long periods of time. Distortions in Mexico's financial system prior to 1982 were relatively limited; however, financial repression emerged after 1982 when inflation surged and interest rate ceilings persisted, and the banking system was nationalized.

[84]In India, reforms of the nonbank financial sector (including equity and insurance markets) have been more extensive. See Chopra and others (1995).

[85]See Bisat and others (1992).

tempted to increase competition in the financial sector. Although it is difficult to establish a direct empirical link, the post-reform period did witness a marked financial deepening.

Mexico provides a similar lesson. The high margins of financial intermediation,[86] reflecting inefficient bank operations, lack of competition, and the deterioration in the quality of bank portfolios in recent years, seriously hindered the private sector's investment response.

---

[86]This assessment is based on World Bank (1994b).

• Inadequate public enterprise reform can be a major obstacle to the development of efficient financial intermediation. The experience of Bangladesh is particularly illustrative. The persistent high proportion of nonperforming loans in bank portfolios—largely stemming from a weak public enterprise sector—widened interest rate spreads; the consequent high lending rates appear to be a major factor accounting for the muted response of private investment to adjustment policies and may have dampened the productivity response. Similar factors appear to be at work, to varying degrees, in Ghana, India, and Senegal.

IX Role of Labor Markets

The structure of labor markets can have a major impact on the transmission of adjustment policies to investment and growth, and the policies themselves also influence labor market developments. This section examines the links between adjustment policies and labor markets by first identifying some salient labor market features and then by examining, to the extent that the limited data permit, the impact of adjustment policies on real wages and employment in the eight countries.[87]

Structure of Labor Markets

Three labor market features, shared more or less by all eight countries, are especially relevant for the impact of adjustment policies (Appendix V, Table 22 summarizes the labor market characteristics and reforms in each of these countries). First, labor markets are often segmented—between regulated formal markets and unregulated, often much larger, informal markets; between urban and rural sectors; and between public and private sectors.[88] Although segmentation may arise from many factors, government regulation and unionization play a critical role. Laws against dismissal of workers or regulations requiring generous severance payments, mandatory wage increases, minimum wages, or other requirements that imply large nonwage labor costs not only create substantial fixed costs to hiring and reduce wage flexibility but also discourage the employment and real-location of labor in the formal sector.[89] In contrast,

regulations are either nonexistent or poorly enforced in most informal markets. Second, some labor markets are characterized by the extensive role of the public sector, as reflected by the large share of public sector employment in formal markets and/or high public sector wages (India, Bangladesh, Ghana, Morocco, and Senegal). Public sector wage awards that are not linked to productivity gains exert pressure on private sector wages in the formal sector and have an important leverage effect on wage costs. Third, labor markets can be characterized by a high degree of indexation that tends to introduce rigidity into the setting of real wages (for example, Chile before 1982).

One striking observation is that the basic regulatory structure and other institutional features of labor markets have changed little in most of the eight countries during the course of adjustment. Moreover, with the exception of public sector wages and employment, there was typically limited mention of such issues in most IMF-supported programs in these countries. Chile is the only case where major labor market reforms were undertaken. Although public service reform was recognized as important in Bangladesh, Senegal, and Ghana, actions generally fell short of original goals. In Mexico, labor market reforms were limited and lagged behind other structural reforms. In contrast to the other seven countries, Thailand's labor markets remained relatively free of institutional restrictions from the outset of adjustment.

The Impact of Adjustment Policies on Real Wages and Relative Prices

The response of real wages influences how adjustment policies affect investment, output, and employment. Real wage flexibility (measured in terms of traded goods prices) is needed for a nominal devaluation to result in a real exchange rate depreciation and a transfer of resources to the tradable goods sector. A broad indication of relative real wage developments can be obtained through two measures of changes in "wage-gaps." The first captures the

---

[87]These issues are also discussed in Agénor and Aizenman (1994) and in World Bank (1995).

[88]Segmentation does not imply independence; shocks in one submarket can have significant wage and employment repercussions in the others.

[89]For example, stringent job security regulations in India (including the requirement in most cases to obtain prior government consent for layoffs) are estimated to reduce formal employment in 35 industries by 18 percent (World Bank (1995)). In Morocco, temporary employment in manufacturing grew two and a half times faster than permanent employment in 1984–90 largely because of restrictions against layoffs (World Bank (1994c)). See also Tahari and others (forthcoming) for a discussion of regulations in Senegal.

difference between the growth of actual real wages and that warranted by productivity growth; a positive value thus has negative implications for employment and output. The second is based on the growth of unit labor costs relative to that of trading partners; a positive value indicates a decline in competitiveness (Chart 21).[90]

The effectiveness of exchange rate policy in bringing about a reduction in real wages and a depreciation of the real exchange rate depends on many factors, particularly the adoption of consistent macroeconomic policies. As noted in Section IV, the indexation of nominal wages can be especially important. For instance, the indexation of wages to past inflation in Chile (1978–82), together with a fixed exchange rate, contributed to a sharp increase in real wages and an unsustainable real appreciation that eventually led to a severe contraction of output and investment in 1982–83 and massive unemployment. However, following the elimination of mandatory backward wage indexation in 1982 and the shift to a flexible exchange rate regime, Chile was able to lower real wages sharply and effect a real effective exchange rate depreciation of some 50 percent by 1985–87. At the same time, it maintained low inflation and generated substantial growth in output and employment. The persistence of considerable unemployment for several years must also have put downward pressure on real wages. In line with these developments, Chart 21 shows that, prior to 1982, real wage growth exceeded that of warranted wages while relative unit labor costs increased substantially; this relationship reversed in the mid-1980s.

Mexico's experience suggests that forward-looking wage agreements can be useful in breaking inflation inertia, but it is also indicative of the difficulties that may arise to adequately assess a country's external competitiveness especially during periods of considerable structural transformation; in such circumstances, labor market rigidities are likely to be of particular importance. While real wages grew broadly in line with warranted wages, Mexico's relative unit labor costs picked up appreciably from 1988 onward (Chart 21). To a considerable extent this reflected the reversal of an earlier substantial depreciation in the real exchange rate.[91] The surge in

capital inflows during the early 1990s was clearly a major factor underlying this development and, in practice, it would have been difficult for exchange rate or wage policies alone to fully offset the effects of these inflows. Nevertheless, even though productivity growth was strong in the manufacturing sector, labor market reforms, aimed at addressing structural rigidities in the labor market at an early stage, could have enhanced competitiveness.

Of course, the degree of indexation itself is likely to be conditioned by past experience with inflation. A history of relatively low inflation and stable macroeconomic policies, as in Thailand, is typically associated with relatively flexible labor markets so that nominal exchange rate policy can be effective in bringing about a sustained real depreciation. Thus, the nominal exchange rate depreciations of the mid-1980s brought about a substantial improvement in Thailand's relative unit labor costs—an improvement that was maintained in later years as real wage growth after 1987 was generally at, or below, the warranted rate suggested by productivity improvements.[92] In Morocco, which had a history of generally moderate inflation, adjustment measures, including devaluation and fiscal tightening, reduced real wage growth below productivity growth and thereby improved competitiveness especially during 1984–86. However, real wages and relative unit labor costs rose subsequently, particularly after the exchange rate was pegged in 1990.[93]

The prominence of public sector employment in the formal sector can mitigate the impact of adjustment policies on real wages. In Senegal, real wages in the formal sector remained uncompetitive after adjustment, largely because of high public sector salaries. Similarly, in Ghana, the compensation policies of the Government, which is the largest employer, have tended to limit the responsiveness of formal sector wages to changing market conditions and dampened the output response to adjustment policies (Husain and Faruqee (1994)).

Nevertheless, even in situations where wages in formal markets are rigid, a large informal sector may

---

[90]Because of data limitations, this analysis could only be carried out for Chile, Mexico, Morocco, and Thailand.

[91]In terms of relative unit labor costs in manufacturing, the cumulative real appreciation during 1987–93 amounted to about 80 percent—albeit from a level that was substantially depreciated. This returned the real exchange rate to a level at or above that prevailing in 1983. A similar trend is revealed by other measures of the real exchange rate. Assessments of Mexico's competitiveness during this period have been the subject of considerable controversy, also due to the fact that the marked opening up of the economy, in response to trade and other structural reforms as well

as the increasing integration of the North American economies, led to widely divergent movements in trade indicators. Thus, the real exchange rate appreciation was not enough to discourage strong export growth, but did contribute to a very large increase in import penetration.

[92]The improvement in relative unit labor costs was also partly due to broader regional developments, especially rising labor costs in Japan, Korea, and Taiwan Province of China. See Kochhar and others (forthcoming).

[93]These calculations are based on formal sector employment and total manufacturing output. Over time, the share of the formal sector in total employment appears to have increased reflecting changes in the structure of the economy and deregulation. Therefore, productivity growth may be understated and changes in unit labor costs and the wage gap overstated.

Chart 21. Wages, Productivity, and Unit Labor Costs
(In percentage points)

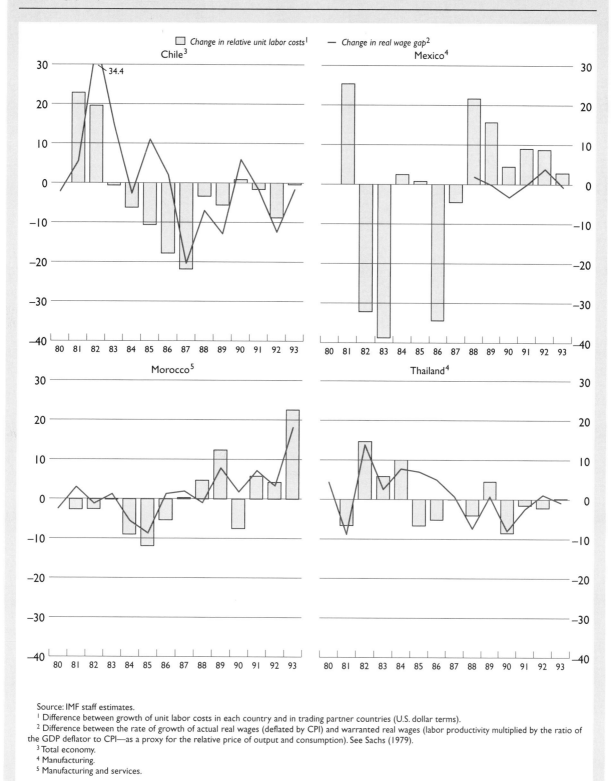

Source: IMF staff estimates.
[1] Difference between growth of unit labor costs in each country and in trading partner countries (U.S. dollar terms).
[2] Difference between the rate of growth of actual real wages (deflated by CPI) and warranted real wages (labor productivity multiplied by the ratio of the GDP deflator to CPI—as a proxy for the relative price of output and consumption). See Sachs (1979).
[3] Total economy.
[4] Manufacturing.
[5] Manufacturing and services.

make it easier for adjustment policies to bring about substantial changes in relative prices, including the real exchange rate. Thus, in India and Bangladesh, where the formal sector is small relative to the total labor market, most of the adjustment to nominal exchange rate changes takes place through a reduction of real informal sector wages. Similarly, in Ghana, real wage flexibility that reflects the relatively large informal sector has facilitated the sectoral reallocations sought by the Economic Recovery Program (Horton and others (1994)). This does, however, raise questions of efficiency and equity since the burden of adjustment placed on informal sector wages is likely to be even greater.[94]

The Impact of Adjustment Policies on Employment and Unemployment

Even when adjustment policies succeed in lowering real wages and shifting relative prices, the speed and extent of the employment response depends on the elasticities of employment with respect to output and real wages.[95] These, in turn, would be influenced by the mobility of labor across sectors and the substitutability of labor for other factors of production. The limited evidence available indicates a fairly strong relationship between employment and output both during the course of adjustment (Chart 22), particularly if the formal sector is relatively large (Chile, Mexico, and Morocco) or if labor market segmentation is limited (Thailand); in these cases, policies that have fostered (or impeded) a strong output response have typically had a similar impact on employment. By contrast, in Bangladesh and, even more notably, in India, formal sector employment has been relatively static, even at times of substantial output fluctuation, mainly because of institutional rigidities. In these latter countries, labor market adjustment appears to have taken place largely through a reduction in real wages in the informal market.

The elasticity of employment with respect to output can be affected by the composition of output as well as relative prices. Although data limitations do not permit a more systematic analysis, the evidence from some of the country case studies is indicative. In Chile, the reduction in real wages eventually (that is, by the mid-1980s) generated an expansion of output in relatively labor-intensive sectors and firms and also induced the use of more labor in the production process. The lag in employment expansion is partly attributable to the fact that a large proportion of exports was based on natural resources and dominated by relatively capital-intensive large firms. Similarly, in Morocco, the large decline in real wages during the early and mid-1980s led to a marked rise in employment after 1985, aided by the expansion of labor-intensive, export-oriented manufacturing following trade liberalization.[96] In Senegal, because of the rigidities in the formal sector, the manufacturing supply response shifted to the informal sector in the latter half of the 1980s; consequently, the decline in formal employment appears to have been offset by job creation in the informal sector. In Ghana, agricultural employment increased markedly with the Economic Recovery Program. Finally, the employment response in Bangladesh was dampened by the prominence of the public sector in the production of cotton and jute textiles.[97]

Unemployment data, and even the notion of unemployment, have to be interpreted with care in many of the eight countries. The absence of formal social safety nets does not permit prolonged periods of open unemployment in informal markets. Underemployment and sporadic employment are much more common and are not accurately captured by the data. Available information suggests that labor market segmentation and the relative size of the for-

---

[94]For instance, model simulations for Bangladesh indicate that when formal sector wages are rigid, a real depreciation raises real wages in the formal sector and reduces them in the informal sector because unemployed formal sector workers expand the supply of informal sector labor (World Bank (1995)). Also, there are signs that real wages in India's informal sector fell during the 1991–92 adjustment period, although observers attribute much of this decline to a relatively poor harvest.

[95]The lack of adequate data makes it difficult to analyze the effect of adjustment policies on employment and unemployment (particularly for Ghana and Senegal). Because data on informal markets are unavailable, measured employment in most cases refers only to formal sector employment.

[96]Evidence on the impact of trade liberalization on labor markets is mixed. In a review of the literature, Agénor (1995) notes that in Morocco, trade reform is estimated to have had a small, but notable, impact on employment and wages in manufacturing during 1984–90, with pronounced sectoral shifts in employment (Currie and Harrison (1994)). The evidence on Mexico, appears inconclusive: according to Revenga (1995), tariff reduction (of about 10 percentage points) between 1985–88 reduced manufacturing employment by 2–3 percentage points and increased average wages, with marked intraindustry shifts in employment; however, Feliciano (1994) finds no employment impact and an increase in wage dispersion rather than an effect on average wages. In both Mexico and Morocco, the increase in wages may have reflected a change in the composition of employment toward highly skilled high-wage workers.

[97]Model-based simulations for Bangladesh indicate that an increase in output-employment elasticities (for example, through labor market reform) would significantly reduce the extent of underemployment (World Bank (1995)).

Chart 22. Employment, Unemployment, and Output
(Annual changes; in percent unless otherwise specified)

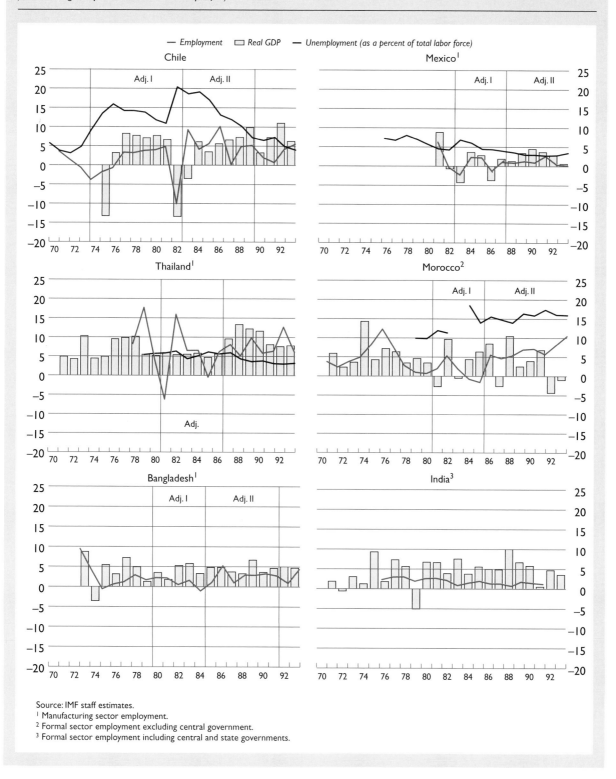

Source: IMF staff estimates.
[1] Manufacturing sector employment.
[2] Formal sector employment excluding central government.
[3] Formal sector employment including central and state governments.

mal market influences the increase in open unemployment during adjustment.[98] In some situations, as in Mexico (1981–82) and Chile (1982–83), where formal labor markets are relatively large, a sharp increase in unemployment appears to have precipitated the fall in real wages (see Chart 22). By contrast, in Thailand, where labor markets are relatively flexible and segmentation is quite low, and in India and Bangladesh, where informal markets are relatively large, the reduction in real wages was achieved without a sharp increase in unemployment. In Morocco, although employment increased from 1986 to 1993, the entry into the labor force of increasing numbers of young, relatively more educated workers resulted in an increase in open unemployment.

---

[98]For instance, the World Bank (1995) estimates that underemployment in Bangladesh is widespread and equivalent to having more than one fourth of the labor force unemployed. In India, Morocco, and Thailand, open unemployment is concentrated on younger and better educated workers (who are supported by other means), while in Chile a large proportion of unemployed in the 1980s were skilled workers.

X Conclusions and Lessons for Program Design

A number of questions stem from the central issue of why the response of investment and growth to adjustment policies was often slow. This section poses those questions, summarizes the principal messages emerging from the country studies, and outlines the lessons for the design of adjustment policies. These messages not only are relevant for IMF-supported adjustment programs but also point to issues that are central to the IMF's surveillance role. In discussing these questions, however, the limitations of the methodological approaches that are utilized, which are discussed in more detail in the introduction, should be recognized. In particular, while the use of case studies provides an opportunity for a more in-depth examination of the effects of policies, it is difficult to establish the robustness and generality of conclusions based on evidence from only a small group of countries.

The experience of the eight countries supports the broad consensus that follows and that is also derived from a wide variety of other studies that are summarized in Appendix I: (1) the objectives of a sustainable external position, moderate inflation, and faster economic growth are likely to be mutually reinforcing over the medium term; and (2) getting certain fundamental policies right—prudent fiscal and monetary management, creating effective and secure financial systems, investing heavily in human capital (especially basic education), limiting domestic price distortions (especially to ensure that the domestic relative prices of traded goods remain close to international levels), and promoting flexible labor markets—builds the foundations for, but does not guarantee, sustained growth.

Going beyond this broad consensus to consider the problems of a transition to a policy environment conducive to growth, two central themes emerge. First, because of the forward-looking nature of investment and saving decisions, market assessments of the internal consistency and sustainability of policies greatly influence the size and speed with which private investment and saving respond to adjustment measures. Consequently, the indirect effects of second-best policy choices—through reduced confidence inducing investors to wait and see or through

disruptions to intertemporal consumption choices because new policies are expected to be temporary—may be greater, although harder to predict, than their direct macroeconomic effects. Second, in each country there appear to be close links between particular aspects of macroeconomic and structural reforms that are likely to be mutually supporting. Therefore, the notion of a "critical mass" of reforms does appear to be important, even though the key linkages are likely to be country-specific and difficult to establish robustly. This judgment is reinforced by one of the conclusions of the companion fiscal study, which emphasizes that systemic reforms of the tax and public expenditure management structures are likely to be essential components of a growth-oriented fiscal policy, whatever the pattern of expenditure reduction or tax increases initially adopted as part of the stabilization effort.[99]

Were the episodes of sharp declines in investment and growth and the subsequent slow recovery inevitable?

The severity of the decline in output and investment as well as the speed of recovery depended upon how promptly adjustment was initiated. No country in the study that postponed adjustment until faced with severe macroeconomic instability and external crisis avoided a substantial decline in investment and a slowdown in growth. Indeed, the evidence from the case studies and from cross-country analysis suggests that periods of severe macroeconomic instability are especially harmful to investment and growth and that some of these harmful effects are likely to linger even after adjustment begins. The reasons, not all of which are easily quantifiable, appear to include the rational "wait and see" attitude of private investors when faced with increased uncertainty and the difficulty of establishing stable relative price signals, including those for the exchange rate and interest rates. Policies undertaken in crisis conditions sometimes included ad hoc or emergency measures that were not conducive to growth. Therefore, in countries in which a withdrawal of external financ-

---

[99]Mackenzie and others (forthcoming).

ing, and a consequent sharp turnaround in the direction of net resource transfers, forced an abrupt contraction in domestic absorption, the impact fell heavily on investment, both private and public, and typically gave insufficient time for resources to switch from the nontradable to tradable goods sectors. Private investment generally fell more steeply in such episodes than can be explained by traditional macroeconomic determinants.

Moreover, the case studies generally support the judgment that the response of the economy to policy measures may differ, and be harder to predict, during episodes of macroeconomic crisis; for example, "crowding-in" effects, which would tend to offset the direct contractionary impact of fiscal consolidation, are likely to be weaker and slower to operate in conditions of economic uncertainty. In these circumstances, policies that minimize the damage to growth are likely to be those that begin an early restoration of internal and external stability and avoid actions—such as a widespread intensification of controls or measures of a confiscatory nature—that further undermine private sector confidence. Typically, the recovery in investment following such a crisis took several years; such investment "pauses" have also been identified in a number of other studies, discussed in Appendix I. The contrasting experience of Thailand, which also encountered substantial external shocks prior to its adjustment, reinforces the view that a strategy of early corrective action to emerging macroeconomic imbalances enhances growth.

Two important lessons for IMF operations stem from these observations.

• As an economy emerges from such a crisis, there are limits to what adjustment policies can achieve in the short term. Evidence on IMF-supported programs in the eight countries suggests some tendency to overestimate the speed of private investment recovery—although unanticipated exogenous factors and policy slippages probably also played a role.

• Since a good "track record" of macroeconomic adjustment appears to make adjustment less costly, the role of surveillance is central to the IMF's contribution to improving growth prospects—through detecting, and encouraging authorities to address, imbalances at an early stage.

How did macroeconomic policies enhance or impede the recovery in investment and growth?

The individual country studies suggest that the sustainability and consistency of policies are likely to be central in preventing expectations of policy reversal from potentially locking an economy into a low-investment, low-growth equilibrium. In a number of cases, potential inconsistencies between different components of the adjustment effort (for example, between exchange rate, fiscal, and wage policies, or between the goals of fiscal consolidation and certain structural reforms) appear to have contributed to weakening the supply response and sometimes led to policy reversals.

The fiscal position is usually critical. The fiscal adjustment has to be strong enough both to minimize the burden placed on interest rates and private credit, and hence private investment, and also to support any needed adjustment in the real exchange rate. However, expectations about the future course of fiscal policy are likely to be critical to the transmission process. The importance of considering the budget in a multiperiod framework is also supported by the results of the companion study on the composition of fiscal adjustment, since certain reforms may entail a trade-off between deficit reduction now and deficit reduction in the future.[100] One possible benchmark of fiscal sustainability that is considered in the present study is the primary balance that would be consistent with maintaining a constant public debt-to-GDP ratio in the context of low inflation and no financial repression. The results suggest that judgments about the sustainability of fiscal policy based on such a debt dynamics criterion do not necessarily imply that fiscal policy is consistent with other macroeconomic objectives, notably for growth and the external current account. In particular, the case studies suggest that the linkages between fiscal and external imbalances can be difficult to quantify in view of possible changes in private sector saving and investment behavior at a time of substantial changes in macroeconomic and structural policies.

In most of the eight countries, the evidence from econometric estimates of the determinants of investment suggests that efforts to rationalize public investment programs did not, on balance, discourage private investment. Indeed, withdrawal from sectors where public investment competed with private sector opportunities often appear to have generated a positive investment response. However, this does not mean that public investment in basic infrastructure, health, and education was not crucial to growth. The findings also suggest that ensuring an adequate flow of credit to the private sector, including through the removal of credit constraints, is likely to promote a faster recovery of investment.

The country case studies also reaffirm the message emerging from previous empirical work that raising public saving is likely to be the most effective means of raising total saving in the economy.

Policies to promote resource switching are necessary to minimize the initial output contraction fol-

---

[100]Mackenzie and others (forthcoming).

lowing stabilization and to provide adequate incentives for investment in export and import-competing activities. The speed with which such switching occurs depends upon the coordination of exchange rate, fiscal, and labor market policies and their impact on the real exchange rate. The experiences of Chile (in 1978–82) and Mexico (after 1988) suggest that consistency among policies is especially important in influencing the trade-off with external competitiveness when the exchange rate is used as the main nominal anchor in a rapid disinflation strategy. Fiscal correction and removal of backward wage indexation both appear to be important in breaking inflation inertia, but even then the short-term consequences for aggregate demand and the external current account are hard to predict, especially when trade and financial sector reforms are under way at the same time. The likelihood of an unsustainable real appreciation and consumption boom, followed by a late recession, can be reduced if fiscal policy remains geared toward controlling demand pressures and the anchoring strategy gives way to greater exchange rate flexibility, perhaps in the form of a one-time devaluation, once disinflation objectives have largely been achieved.

Lessons for the design of IMF-supported programs include the following:

• Programs should contain an explicit evaluation of fiscal sustainability in the context of a forward-looking medium-term framework, and such assessments need to take account of private sector responses to the adjustment effort; since these responses cannot be predicted with accuracy, the trade-offs involved need to be kept under close review.

• More generally, a recurrent theme is the difficulty of predicting accurately the response of some key macroeconomic variables, such as private saving and investment and the external current account, to adjustment policies. This underscores the importance of program reviews, and of surveillance activities during and after the program, not only to assess whether announced policies are on track but also to provide the opportunity for a more fundamental reappraisal of whether assumptions on key relationships underlying the macroeconomic framework remain valid.

• As for saving, some IMF-supported programs in the eight countries appear to have taken insufficient account of the partial offset in private saving that typically occurs when public saving is raised and therefore tended to be overoptimistic about saving developments. Program projections for private saving should take careful account of the available empirical evidence on the determinants of saving in each country, but such projections are inherently subject to wide margins of error at times of consider-

able structural change. Consequently, the medium-term framework should be revamped if the outcome for private saving is significantly lower than assumed; in these circumstances, a larger increase in public saving may need to be targeted to achieve the authorities' growth and external objectives.

• The mix of fiscal and monetary policies should ensure an adequate supply of credit to the private sector since this is crucial to a rapid investment response. Moreover, consistency of fiscal policies and disinflation objectives is necessary to reduce uncertainty, irrespective of the nominal anchor being used. Although these issues are already a central concern of IMF-supported programs, it would be useful to address more explicitly in program documents the assumed links between credit availability, interest rates, and private investment that underlie program design. Furthermore, program design needs to deal explicitly with the problems of weak bank portfolios.

How did the design of structural reforms improve or impede growth prospects?

Although the complex nature of structural reforms makes it difficult to establish precise quantitative links with productivity and investment, the weight of evidence from the case studies supports the judgment that the elimination of major distortions fosters higher growth. It is not possible to extract from the case studies a single comprehensive blueprint on the design and sequencing of structural reforms; indeed, in countries where the supply response was strongest governments did not always follow what are generally regarded as "best practices" (for example, in trade and financial sector reforms). Nevertheless, in each country there were particular aspects of structural reform where strong complementarities existed. This suggests that implementation of an internally consistent core set of reforms is likely to minimize the risks of policy reversals and, by signaling their credibility and sustainability, to maximize the beneficial impact on growth. However, the nature of these critical links can vary from country to country, so program design needs to take careful account of individual country circumstances.

Eliciting a strong supply response to reforms also depends importantly upon overall consistency with supporting financial, exchange rate, and wage policies. For example, even in Chile, where reforms began early and were the most wide-ranging, the full benefits for growth were delayed by policies that contributed to an unsustainable exchange rate appreciation and external current account deficits during the early 1980s.

The "core" set of reforms is inevitably country specific, but key complementarities that emerged in a number of the country cases include the following:

• Trade reforms that were accompanied by broader tax reforms were more likely to be sustained. Where quantitative trade and exchange restrictions were extensive, their early removal appears to have helped the supply response as well as easing the potential trade-off between fiscal consolidation and tariff reduction.

• Problems with the quality of bank balance sheets appear to have been a major impediment to the response of private investment in a number of cases—because of the consequent high intermediation costs—and sometimes gave rise to severe financial crises that exacerbated recessions. For these reasons, early attention to strengthening prudential regulation and supervision is crucial. Difficulties in effectively enforcing an announced hardening of budget constraints on public enterprises was a major cause of the problem of nonperforming loans (for example, in Bangladesh, Ghana, and Senegal), which suggests that efforts to restructure and recapitalize the banking system are unlikely to yield their full benefits unless accompanied by effective public enterprise reform and privatization.[101]

• In general, the design of structural policies should emphasize early technical preparation and implementation. Certain broader structural reforms need to be accompanied by and closely coordinated with sector-specific reforms. Important examples of such linkages are (1) agricultural pricing and marketing reforms to complement trade reform, and (2) establishment of a clear legal and institutional framework to accompany broader deregulation of the economy and a scaling back of the public enterprise sector. In a number of cases, insufficient emphasis on or delays in implementing sectoral-level and institutional measures appear to have dampened the supply response to structural reforms. Design and implementation of these reforms generally took a long time and often lagged behind the broader reforms, which suggests that they should be initiated early in the adjustment process. This evidence also underscores the importance of close coordination between the IMF and the World Bank on structural issues.

How has the structure of labor markets influenced the response of output and employment to adjustment?

Although the quality of information on labor market developments in the eight countries varies substantially, their experience generally suggests that the degree of flexibility in labor markets can have a major influence on the speed and size of the output and employment response to policies.

With the exception of Thailand, all of the countries began the adjustment process with significant rigidities involving, to varying degrees, one or more of the following features: segmented labor markets with regulated formal sectors that limit wage flexibility and discourage the reallocation of labor between the formal and informal sectors; the extensive role of the public sector in employment and wage-setting in the formal sector; and a high degree of wage indexation (most notably Chile until 1982). However, with the marked exception of Chile, features of labor markets in the eight countries have been very difficult to change. Moreover, in a few other countries (Ghana and Senegal) in which labor market reform was identified as a major element of adjustment, actions typically fell well short of expectations.

Nevertheless, in a number of countries, labor market reform appears to offer considerable potential to increase the flexibility of real wages and raise the elasticity of employment with respect to output. The limited evidence available suggests a fairly strong association between output and employment in countries where the formal sector is large or labor market segmentation is limited (as in Thailand). In countries with large informal sectors, institutional rigidities have typically meant that the main burden of adjustment has fallen on wages in the informal sector—although the patchy nature of the data makes this difficult to confirm.

Wage indexation arrangements can have an important influence on the short-term path of output following the implementation of disinflation strategies. A clear example is Chile, where the exceptional severity of the 1975 and 1982–83 recessions (following money-based and exchange-rate-based stabilization efforts, respectively) appears to have been due in part to the prevalence of backward-looking wage indexation. For example, the failure to change indexation arrangements during 1978–82, when the exchange rate was used as an anchor for the price level, contributed to a sharp increase in real wages, excess demand pressures, and an unsustainable real appreciation that led eventually to a severe contraction of output and employment. By contrast, following the elimination of mandatory indexation in 1982 and the shift to a flexible exchange rate regime, real wages were lowered sharply and Chile was able to effect a large real exchange rate depreciation without reigniting inflation, thereby helping to lay the foundation for a period of sustained growth in output and employment.[102]

---

[101]Public enterprise reforms are discussed in the companion study by Mackenzie and others (forthcoming).

[102]A number of other factors, including the fiscal policy stance, were also important; these two episodes are discussed at greater length in Section IV.

The experience of the eight countries suggests two labor market issues deserving of particular attention in the design of adjustment programs:

• Institutional arrangements affecting the extent and nature of wage indexation should be an important consideration in the design of disinflation strategies. The extent of de facto or de jure wage indexation influences the effectiveness of policy instruments such as the nominal exchange rate and should be addressed explicitly in program design, especially when wage-price inertia is high, whatever nominal anchor strategy is pursued.

• Labor market rigidities in the eight countries were generally given limited attention in program design. Their experience suggests that programs would benefit from a greater integration of such issues into the overall macroeconomic and structural framework. However, such rigidities have typically been one of the most difficult areas in which to bring about fundamental change.

How important was the availability of external financing for growth?

It has generally been difficult to identify a robust association between external financing and growth because of the endogeneity of most financing and because policies and financing interact in complex ways. Nevertheless, the partial evidence available from the country studies suggests that the timely availability of additional financing can enhance growth prospects.

Confidence factors associated with the debt crisis and the authorities' initial policy response appear to have been important factors behind the fall in private investment in countries that encountered severe debt-servicing difficulties. In some (for example, Mexico), the large switch from external to domestic financing by the public sector that followed the debt crisis appears to have squeezed credit available for the private sector, despite substantial fiscal adjustment. Although an independent effect of debt overhang indicators on investment could not be identified for most countries, this certainly does not imply that the debt crisis and the associated sudden and large shift in net resource transfers abroad did not have a major adverse influence on investment. Rather, such effects operate primarily through other variables, including interest rates and credit availability; indeed, there is some evidence to indicate that the resolution of debt and debt-servicing issues was associated with a reduction in interest rates. The beneficial effects on output arising from a relaxation of financing constraints also appear to have been important in those cases (most notably Ghana but also India) where previous delays in adjustment had led to severe constraints on imported intermediate inputs. However, higher growth did not occur in all

countries in which inflows of official or private capital picked up; the most lasting effects appear to have occurred in countries in which fiscal and structural policies favored the channeling of the additional financing toward increased investment, especially in tradables.

Although the impact of external financing is manifold, the country cases point to the following general observation:

• Provided the right supporting policies are in place, the timely availability of additional financing is likely to strengthen growth, and the beneficial effects can be especially important following periods when financing was sharply constrained.

What distinguishes countries that appear to have been successful in achieving a transition to faster growth and what lessons do they suggest?

The linkages between policies and growth are often indirect and can operate with significant and variable lags. Two countries—Chile and Thailand—appear to have made the transition to a more rapid growth path. In addition, in Ghana output recovered sharply, although investment and private saving have yet to make the transition to a path consistent with sustained rapid growth. Many factors other than policies have an impact on growth. The initial rebound in Chile partly reflected a recovery from a massive recession; Ghana's recovery undoubtedly arose from, in part, the reversal of disastrous policies prior to adjustment; and some of Thailand's growth performance can be attributed to the benefits of being part of a rapidly growing, dynamic region. Consequently, short-term developments in output may not be a good criterion for judging the contribution of adjustment programs to longer-term growth.

Nevertheless, it is clear from the country case studies that macroeconomic and structural policies matter for growth and that a consistent track record of stable macroeconomic policies and nondistortionary structural policies aimed at fostering the private sector as the engine of growth offers the best prospects for sustained medium-term growth. Although there is no single comprehensive blueprint that links the cases of Chile and Thailand—indeed, important aspects of their economic histories have been strikingly different over the past two decades—some common elements are noteworthy.[103]

• Macroeconomic stabilization was generally achieved in a manner that was internally consistent and sustainable; in particular, both countries attained

---

[103]For a comprehensive discussion of economic developments and policies, see Bosworth and others (1994) and Little and others (1993) for Chile, and Kochhar and others (forthcoming) for Thailand.

fiscal deficits that were consistent with moderate inflation and a sustainable external position.

• The combination of exchange rate and domestic financial and labor market policies yielded a real exchange rate that provided adequate incentives for the tradable goods sectors. In Thailand, these two elements were present almost from the outset, while in Chile they were achieved only after painful mistakes that delayed the transition to faster growth.

• Structural reforms were successful in establishing an overall institutional framework to foster the private sector as the engine of growth and in generating consistent and stable relative price signals; in Thailand, these basic elements were present from the beginning and were consistently maintained even though additional reforms were relatively modest.

• As indicated in the companion study,[104] public sector reform also seems to have been the most con-

---

[104]Mackenzie and others (forthcoming).

ducive to growth in the two countries, although their experience also suggests that the path to high-quality fiscal adjustment can take different forms: Chile achieved a radical transformation of its budgetary, pension, and public enterprise systems while managing to protect education and health spending; Thailand began its adjustment with a relatively well-oriented public sector and, although there are some indications that cuts in capital spending may have contributed to infrastructural bottlenecks, the real resources devoted to (especially primary) education and health were increased substantially.

• The flexible operation of labor markets in Thailand and the eventual, albeit difficult and costly (in terms of unemployment), achievement of greater flexibility in Chile were also important factors.

• The stable macroeconomic and regulatory environment encouraged substantial inflows of foreign capital and policies were aimed at directing the inflows to investment rather than consumption.

Appendix I Lessons from Earlier Studies

There is a reasonable degree of consensus on the basic paradigm underlying structural adjustment: macroeconomic stability along with market-based and outward-oriented economic policies are conducive to sustained faster growth—even if such policies are not always sufficient. The experience of the high-growth economies of East Asia also suggests that getting certain fundamental policies right builds the foundation for sustained growth (Box 7). However, the problems of transition to such a growth-friendly policy environment are often not clear-cut and sometimes require difficult trade-offs between intermediate objectives. These choices can be especially complex when, as is the case for most countries undertaking IMF-supported adjustment programs, the initial position is one of severe external financing constraints, large macroeconomic imbalances, and deeply entrenched structural weaknesses. What lessons does experience suggest about managing the transition? Without attempting a comprehensive survey or setting out in detail estimated quantitative relationships, this appendix summarizes some central messages to emerge from some recent studies (denoted by abbreviations in Box 8).

Do Adjustment Policies Foster Growth?

It is extremely difficult to distinguish the effects of adjustment policies from the many other influences on growth in the short term. Indeed, exogenous factors such as the terms of trade are likely to influence not just outcomes but the policies themselves, making it especially hard to disentangle cause and effect. Moreover, the depth and complexity of adjustment programs can vary widely—from short-term macroeconomic stabilization to efforts to address deep-rooted macroeconomic and structural imbalances—so that the lack of a simple association between "adjustment" and growth is hardly surprising. With these caveats, most studies that have examined the effects of adjustment supported by the IMF or the World Bank typically suggest that, on average, real GDP growth was broadly unchanged *(CR)* or

strengthened, albeit only moderately *(RAL-2, RAL-3, and Corbo)*, in the years immediately following the adoption of adjustment programs.[105]

Experience also suggests that delaying core reforms until macroeconomic imbalances and price distortions are well entrenched is likely to be harmful to growth. In particular, there is evidence that growth falls substantially during periods of high inflation and recovers after inflation is stabilized.[106] However, macroeconomic adjustment is not always sufficient to put countries onto a sustained faster growth path. Especially for the low-income countries, long-run development problems associated with weak social and economic infrastructure and institutions still need to be tackled; resolving these problems will require considerable time *(RAL-2, RAL-3, ESAF)*. Nonetheless, the record of adjusting countries in sub-Saharan Africa suggests that, even in countries with deep-rooted development constraints, progress toward macroeconomic stability helps to promote growth, both through its effects on productivity and on capital accumulation *(Hadjimichael* and *Africa)*.

In only a few countries (most notably in Asia, such as Korea and Thailand) were episodes of significant adjustment in macroeconomic and structural

---

[105]Khan (1990), using a modified control-group approach that attempts to distinguish between the impact of macroeconomic policies and the Fund program per se, concludes that achievement of macroeconomic stability had a positive impact on long-run growth whereas, after allowing for an estimate of the policy changes that would have taken place even without Fund arrangements, the growth rate declined in the program year. This adverse effect diminished when the time horizon was extended beyond the program year. Mosley and others (1991) identify a weak positive association between Bank-supported programs and GDP growth. Using a similar approach, Conway (1994) concludes that participation in Fund-supported programs had a negative same-year effect on growth and domestic investment, but that the lagged effects were both positive and larger than the same-year effects.

[106] For example, see De Gregorio (1992). Bruno and Easterly (1995) show that this negative relationship between growth and inflation is much more robust at high rates of inflation (that is, annual rates above 40 percent).

Box 7. Lessons from the East Asian "Miracle"

The World Bank's comprehensive study of the factors underlying the success of the eight high-performing Asian economies concluded that there was no single "model" of success.[1] The role of public policy varied from Hong Kong, with its hands-off approach, to much more activist policies in Japan and Korea. However, some common threads do emerge, including a commitment to a relatively equal dispersion of the benefits of growth and a reliance on the private sector. Moreover, getting the fundamentals right in several broad policy areas was crucial: (1) prudent fiscal and monetary management; (2) heavy investment in human capital, especially in basic education; (3) creation of effective and secure financial systems; (4) limiting price distortions, especially to ensure that domestic prices of traded goods were never too far from international prices, and promoting flexible labor markets to help supply respond quickly to those prices; (5) ensuring easy access to foreign technology rather than attempting a path of self-reliance; and (6) limiting the bias of price incentives against agriculture. In countries that relied on selective government intervention, notably in the areas of industrial policy and the financial sector, the results of such intervention were mixed. The study finds that some favorable outcomes were achieved by creating competition among firms to meet well-defined economic performance criteria in return for preferential treatment; even then, industrial policies also produced some notable failures. Moreover, the conditions for successful intervention (notably a bureaucracy insulated from political pressures) would be hard to reproduce and were less crucial to growth than the fundamentals emphasized above.

---

[1] See World Bank (1993b), Chapter 7.

number of years *(RAL-2, Chhibber)*. Even in some of the Asian success cases (for example, Indonesia) the foundations for growth were laid only over quite a long period.[107]

The usual relationship between real GDP growth and the ratio of investment to GDP typically breaks down during adjustment periods. Growth is faster than one would expect given the decline in investment, either because of efficiency improvements associated with adjustment or because of a recovery in capacity utilization *(RAL-2, OED)*.[108]

Investment and Saving: The Need for Credibility and Sound Fiscal Policies

Countries need to establish a track record of sound policies—macroeconomic and structural—before a significant strengthening of private investment can be expected, and this takes time *(CR, RAL-2, RAL-3)*. The investment "pause" can typically last from three to five years in middle-income countries and even longer in many low-income countries *(RAL-3, Chhibber)*.

It is not possible to make general statements about the links between public and private investment; effects vary by country, depending upon the extent to which governments compete with the private sector for investment opportunities and access to financing. For example, crowding-out effects predominate in about half of the cases considered in *Easterly*. However, econometric studies suggest that public infrastructure investment is often positively correlated with private investment.[109]

The channels for policies to directly influence saving rates are often limited. Increasing government saving is the most direct means to raise national saving. On average, only about half of any change in government saving is offset by opposite movements in private saving *(CR, RAL-2, Easterly)*.[110] Haque

policies followed by a swift transition to a new growth path with only a short recession. These countries typically had smaller initial macroeconomic problems and structural distortions, possessed reasonably well-developed private sectors, and generally had above-average growth rates even prior to adjustment. In these cases, exports, saving, and, with a short lag, private investment all rose following the implementation of adjustment policies. For most other countries, structural adjustment has taken longer and has typically involved a period of declining output and labor demand before new sources of growth emerged. Higher exports and saving frequently followed after a year or two (although often only weakly in many low-income countries) but private investment generally only responded after a

---

[107] The long transition from severe distortions to sustained growth in Indonesia is discussed in Woo and others (1994).

[108] Branson and Jayarajah (1995) reach the same conclusion.

[109] Serven and Solimano (1994) and the references therein. The results reported in *Hadjimichael* suggest that, on balance, government investment has generally complemented private investment in sub-Saharan Africa in recent years. However, investment by public enterprises—potentially the most important source of direct crowding-out effects—were included in private investment for the purposes of the study.

[110] The conclusions that fiscal adjustment induces an offset, but only a partial one, in private saving is supported by a large number of econometric studies. See Savastano (1995) and Masson and others (1995) for a discussion of this evidence. The method of raising public saving also appears to matter, with a cut in current spending inducing a smaller decline in private saving than would an increase in tax revenues; see Corbo and Schmidt-Hebbel (1991).

Box 8. Principal Studies Referred to in Appendix I

• *Africa:* World Bank studies focusing on economic reform and adjustment in sub-Saharan Africa; see World Bank (1994a) and Husain and Faruqee (1994).

• *Bruno:* contains case studies of stabilization in a number of high-inflation countries—Argentina, Bolivia, Brazil, Chile, Israel, Mexico, and Turkey; see Bruno and others (1991).

• *Chhibber:* contains case studies of Chile, Colombia, Egypt, Indonesia, Morocco, Turkey, and Zimbabwe; see Chhibber and others (1992).

• *Corbo:* symposium on the effectiveness of adjustment lending by the World Bank and on macroeconomic policies to restore sustainable growth; see Corbo, Fischer, and Webb (1992).

• *CR:* the 1994 review of IMF conditionality; see Schadler and others (1995) and Schadler (1995).

• *East Asia:* World Bank study of the role of public policy in development in eight economies—Hong Kong, Indonesia, Japan, Korea, Malaysia, Singapore, Taiwan Province of China, and Thailand; see World Bank (1993b).

• *Easterly:* studies of the links between fiscal adjustment and macroeconomic performance in ten countries—Argentina, Chile, Colombia, Côte d'Ivoire, Ghana, Mexico, Morocco, Pakistan, Thailand, and Zimbabwe; see Easterly and others (1994).

• *ESAF:* the 1993 review of lending under the IMF's enhanced structural adjustment facility; see Schadler, Rozwadowski, Tiwari, and Robinson (1993).

• *Hadjimichael:* IMF study on growth, saving, and investment in sub-Saharan Africa; see Hadjimichael and others (1995).

• *Kirmani:* contains a comprehensive review of the trade policy content of IMF-supported adjustment programs; see Kirmani and others (1994).

• *Little:* studies of 17 countries—Argentina, Brazil, Cameroon, Chile, Colombia, Costa Rica, Côte d'Ivoire, India, Indonesia, Kenya, Mexico, Morocco, Nigeria, Pakistan, Sri Lanka, Thailand, and Turkey; see Little and others (1993).

• *OED:* the 1980–92 report of the World Bank's Operations Evaluation Department; see World Bank, Operations Evaluation Department (1995).

• *OED-Trade Policy:* study by the World Bank's Operations Evaluation Department; see World Bank, Operations Evaluation Department (1992).[1]

---
[1] See also Thomas, Nash, and others (1991) and Papageorgiou and others (1990).

• *RAL-2* and *RAL-3:* the second and third reviews of adjustment lending by the World Bank; see World Bank (1990) and World Bank (1992).

• *WDR:* the World Bank's 1991 *World Development Report;* see World Bank (1991).

• *WEO:* studies of adjustment and growth in the IMF's *World Economic Outlook;* see International Monetary Fund (1992, 1993a, 1993b, and 1994).

These studies have adopted a wide variety of methodological approaches, including detailed analysis of individual country cases (for example, *Africa, East Asia, Bruno, Little);* modified control-group comparisons that attempt to control for initial conditions and exogenous shocks *(RAL-2, RAL-3, Corbo);* cross-country or time-series econometric analysis of the links between policies and performance (most studies); division of countries into groups according to their growth performance in order to identify any systematic policy differences *(RAL-2, RAL-3, OED-Trade Policy, WEO);* and, for a few specific issues, counterfactual simulations using partial or reduced-form models for particular countries *(Easterly, Bruno).* Although all of these studies provide insights into the links between adjustment and growth, each is subject to some methodological limitations that must be borne in mind when interpreting the results.[2] Nevertheless, a number of broad messages emerge consistently and appear to be robust to different approaches.

---
[2] Before-after comparisons are especially likely to be misleading if exogenous influences are important, and division of countries into groups according to their performance is subject to sample selection bias. Modified control-group approaches are, in principle, a conceptually superior way of comparing the outcomes of IMF- or Bank-supported adjustment programs with what would have happened in the absence of such programs, but the policy reaction functions that underlie some of these approaches may be unstable. Model-based simulations of counterfactuals for particular countries are also not without problems: simple models cannot capture all of the important links between policies and outcomes, particularly when structural policy changes are important, whereas more complex models cannot be estimated empirically for most developing countries. Moreover, the problem of parameter instability across regime changes is always an issue.

---

reflects the presence of liquidity constraints affecting some households. Their results also suggest that developments that ease these liquidity constraints—for example, financial reform that liberalizes access to consumer credit—could be associated with a temporary stimulus to consumption.

Most empirical studies have concluded that the real interest elasticity of total savings is not significantly different from zero. However, Ogaki and others (1996) show that the pattern of saving tends to change once subsistence considerations are satisfied. They find positive interest rate effects that vary with income, but are still small. Moreover, there is considerable evidence that positive real interest rates boost the share of saving intermediated through the financial system, with potentially positive effects on investment efficiency.

Macroeconomic Policies

The correlation of fiscal deficits with any one indicator of macroeconomic imbalance (inflation, real exchange rates, and real interest rates) is low in the short run, because of the great variety of ways in which governments finance their deficits.[111] However, there is substantial evidence that reducing large deficits is good for growth.[112] The benefits can operate through various channels including reduced monetary financing and hence inflation and reduced issuance of domestic debt, which helps reverse crowding out; as well as effects on the exchange rate *(RAL-3, Easterly)*.

At an aggregate level, the composition of fiscal adjustment in IMF-supported programs was typically tailored to the nature of the imbalances: in terms of country averages, deficit reduction was targeted to come equally from revenue increases and expenditure cuts; moreover, targeted revenue increases were largest in countries with low initial revenue ratios. However, ad hoc, mid-program adjustments fell most heavily on expenditures, especially capital spending *(CR)*. Moreover, in many programs supported by the World Bank there has been an inadequate reallocation of spending to some high priority, growth-oriented activities.[113] Critical nonwage operating and maintenance expenditures were often unduly squeezed, while there was typically scant progress in reducing excessive public sector employment *(RAL-3)*.[114] More fundamentally, adjustment programs have had limited success in tackling problems such as the lack of public sector accountability and transparency that are at the core of efficient public expenditure management. Such problems require broader, and long-term, efforts to build institutional capacity *(Africa)*.

There is some evidence of a nonlinear relationship between real interest rates and growth. Moderately positive real interest rates (that is, in the range of 0–5 percent) have been a feature of most countries

with better than average growth, whereas a larger proportion of countries with negative or very high positive real rates have been in the lower-growth categories. However, a few countries recorded strong growth even though very high ex post real interest rates persisted for long periods *(WEO)*.[115] Real interest rates were also considerably less volatile in the successful East Asian economies than in many other regions, reflecting their record of relative macroeconomic stability *(East Asia)*. Cross-sectional studies suggest that the link between moderately positive real interest rates and growth operates largely through influences on the level and efficiency of financial intermediation, rather than on the overall saving rate.

Exchange rate policy typically reflects a tension between two goals: first, anchoring inflation expectations and disciplining fiscal policies; and, second, maintaining or improving competitiveness. Ideally, financial policies would be sufficiently restrictive to allow the exchange rate to be used as an anchor, with adjustment only in the face of real disturbances. In practice, financial policies are usually not this strong, and there is frequently a trade-off between inflation and competitiveness *(CR, Bruno)*. This trade-off is perhaps most evident during exchange-rate-based stabilization where even in "successful" disinflation efforts backed by substantial fiscal consolidation, such as those of Chile and Israel, choices on when or if to relax the anchor can have an important influence on the transition from stabilization to growth—in part because such choices affect the switch of demand to net exports *(Bruno)*. However, similar choices can be required in countries with a record of low inflation that are subject to large external shocks to which fiscal and wage policies are slow to adjust, such as in the CFA franc zone. Therefore, such trade-offs should be recognized explicitly and kept under close review. An exchange rate anchor may have to give way to greater flexibility in the face of adverse terms of trade movements or a protracted loss of competitiveness. However, limits to the effectiveness of nominal depreciations in achieving a real depreciation without appropriate support from fiscal and wage policies must also be recognized. In particular, explicit real exchange rate rules are never a good idea, because of the inflation risks involved in indexing such an important price and the potential for continuous upward pressure on the money supply through the balance of payments if an attempt is made to set the real rate at an inappropriate level *(CR)*.

Stabilization in economies with chronic inflation is likely to be complicated by built-in mechanisms

---

[111] A more extensive discussion of the theoretical and empirical evidence on the role of public sector reform in promoting growth is contained in Mackenzie and others (forthcoming).

[112] Some of this evidence is discussed in Section III.

[113] Countries with Bank-supported structural adjustment programs generally also had arrangements with the IMF.

[114] For example, only a handful of countries in sub-Saharan Africa have succeeded in reducing the number of civil service employees by more than 5 percent since they began structural adjustment *(Africa* (World Bank, 1994a, p. 123)).

[115] See Table 12 in International Monetary Fund (1992).

for mitigating inflation that make it easier to live with inflation and more difficult to gain a consensus for disinflation policies. Even when successful, stabilization is likely to be protracted because of imperfect policy credibility *(Corbo, Bruno)*. If a nominal anchor is used to help break inflationary inertia, both theory and empirical evidence suggest that the choice of anchor can have important effects on the dynamics of the disinflation program. In particular, the timing of any downturn in economic activity associated with the disinflation is typically different for money-based (early recession) and exchange-rate-based (late recession) stabilization episodes.[116] In the case of exchange-rate-based stabilization, imperfect credibility of the anchor and supporting policies frequently leads to an initial, unsustainable boom in consumption and a surge in imports, followed by a recession. In many cases, an additional important factor was the expansionary effects of a repatriation of assets during the initial stages of stabilization. When disinflation efforts have failed, it has often been because of the lack of supporting fiscal policy or an inability to tackle indexation, especially for wages *(CR, Bruno, Corbo)*.[117]

External Financing and the External Economic Environment

It is difficult to identify any systematic association between external financing and growth from cross-country studies.[118] This is not surprising, since the relationship depends crucially on how policies respond to a greater availability of foreign saving. On average, net resource transfers (as a share of GDP) showed little difference between "high-growth" and "low-growth" groups covering all developing countries *(WEO)*.[119] Cross-country evidence provided in *RAL-2* suggests that, on average, total official external flows had a positive effect on growth in low-income countries, but no clear effects for middle-income countries. In sub-Saharan Africa, countries that benefited from an increase in external transfers achieved moderately higher growth rates—although differences in policies were

a more important factor determining growth performance *(Africa)*.[120]

Cross-sectional analysis also provides a mixed picture of the effects of capital flows on investment: the significantly positive relationship between changes in countries' debt-to-GDP ratios and changes in their investment rates that existed during the 1970s suggests that external borrowing tended to raise investment rates; this relationship vanished during 1979–83 and only re-emerged weakly during the rest of the 1980s *(WEO)*. Most econometric results based on cross-section or panel data also support the hypothesis that foreign capital inflows have a negative impact on domestic saving. An IMF staff study of saving behavior suggests that an increase in foreign saving equivalent to 1 percentage point of GDP is associated on average with a decline in national saving of about 0.4 percentage point of GDP.[121] Once again, however, both the *Hadjimichael* and *Africa* studies suggest that the response of policies is crucial: in sub-Saharan Africa, the negative relationship between external financing and domestic saving was much stronger in countries that were not able to address protracted imbalances; indeed, in the group of sustained adjusters, an increase in foreign aid appears to have been associated with a small rise in domestic saving.

Good policies matter for growth, but so does good luck. For example, the "low-growth" group of countries identified in the *WEO* were exposed to a particularly unfavorable external environment during 1984–93.[122] A deteriorating terms of trade and weak industrial country demand is estimated to have reduced the average annual growth rate of this group by ¾ of 1 percentage point during this period, whereas more favorable conditions boosted the average growth rate of the "high-growth" group by 1 percentage point; thus, the external environment accounted for more than one quarter of the difference in growth between the two groups. Nevertheless, even in regions that have been most severely affected by a deteriorating terms of trade—such as sub-Saharan Africa—countries that have acted to improve their competitiveness and implement structural adjustment measures have done better than others in the region in terms of saving, investment, and per capita GDP growth *(Hadjimichael and ESAF)*.

The degree of correlation between external financing and investment or growth appears to differ according to the composition of the external financing.

---

[116] A detailed discussion of recent experiences with nominal anchors in IMF-supported programs is contained in Mecagni (1995). See also Dornbusch and Fischer (1993), Edwards (1993), and Reinhart and Végh (1995).

[117] However, the boom-bust cycle has also occurred in countries that ran fiscal surpluses (for example, Chile in the late 1970s and Israel in 1985–86).

[118] See, for example, Boone (1994).

[119] International Monetary Fund (1993b). The results quoted are for the period 1984–93; similar results have been observed for different time periods.

---

[120] See *Africa* (World Bank, 1994a, Chapter 5). Many of the relationships discussed in this section were not subjected to formal tests of statistical significance.

[121] See International Monetary Fund (1995). The *Africa* and *Hadjimichael* studies reached a similar conclusion.

[122] International Monetary Fund (1994).

Foreign direct investment and private debt-related flows are both more positively correlated with domestic investment than are official flows, whereas foreign direct investment is more positively correlated with real GDP growth than either of the other two types of flows *(WDR)*.[123] However, the direction of causation is not clear: faster growth is also likely to stimulate more foreign direct investment.

Structural Policies: Start Early and Reach a Critical Mass Soon

The analytical basis for comparing different sequences for removing structural distortions in a second-best world is limited; the appropriate sequencing depends on characteristics specific to each case and must, therefore, be based on an evaluation of the main obstacles to growth in each country.[124] Difficult trade-offs between various intermediate goals for structural reform are often required, especially in countries with limited administrative capacity. Nevertheless, the experiences reviewed by the various studies suggest a few general lessons:

Reform efforts must reach a critical mass to be effective. Small reductions in large distortions do little to raise growth; therefore, sequencing should generally begin by tackling the largest distortions *(RAL-2, Corbo, WDR)*.[125]

Structural reforms have typically *not* been successful when they were undertaken without effective macroeconomic stabilization. When macroeconomic conditions are unstable, consumers and producers do not believe the reforms will be sustained; in the resulting uncertainty, their responses can destabilize the reform effort. Moreover, improved resource allocation signals may be lost in the noise created by high inflation *(OED, RAL-2, RAL-3)*.

Reforms that take a long time to be effective should generally begin at an early stage. Moreover, "getting prices right" is not the only determinant of faster growth: supply responses are likely to be muted without comprehensive efforts to address institutional and regulatory bottlenecks, which typically entail long gestation periods *(RAL-3, OED)*. Moreover, there are often close linkages between certain "macro" reforms (such as trade liberalization) and more micro-level, sectoral reforms (such as deregulation of marketing and distribution). Careful attention to the appropriate clustering of such reforms, which can only be determined case by case, can have a major influence on the speed and magnitude of the supply response *(RAL-2, Corbo)*.

The speed of supply response to trade and exchange reforms varies widely from country to country.[126] Reducing protection in the context of a medium-term strategy that clearly establishes and preannounces immediate and medium-term objectives provides the right signals for production and investment and reduces uncertainty, thereby enhancing the supply response and helping to counter pressures for an ad hoc reinstatement of protection. Credibility and sustainability also appear to be enhanced if trade liberalization begins with a substantial initial effort; in contrast, programs that began with weak initial steps are less likely to be sustained *(RAL-2, Corbo, Kirmani)*.[127] Fiscal considerations have often played a key role in limiting the pace of tariff reform, so program design needs to recognize explicitly the link between the two; complementary domestic tax reforms contribute to the sustainability of trade reforms *(Kirmani)*. However, a well-designed trade reform need not be inimical to revenue generation: the conversion of quantitative restrictions to tariffs is likely to increase fiscal revenues and should be implemented at an early stage of macroeconomic stabilization *(Kirmani)*. Poorer and less-diversified economies, often facing institutional weaknesses and impediments to factor mobility, have the slowest supply response to trade reforms; in these cases, efforts to strengthen the base for exports (through domestic regulatory or institutional reforms) often take much longer than expected and should be given high priority *(RAL-2, OED-Trade Policy)*.

Public enterprise reforms, especially divestiture, have typically been among the slowest of all reforms to be implemented, which suggests that the groundwork needs to be laid at an early stage. The primary objective of the reforms should be to improve efficiency, which should not be overshadowed by the short-term goal of generating fiscal receipts from privatization *(OED)*. In Africa, efforts to reform public enterprises through hard budget constraints without privatization have generally not achieved lasting success, because they tend to be undermined by the myriad channels for soft budget support; in such circumstances, removal of explicit budgetary subsidies encouraged their replacement by less-transparent methods *(Africa* (World Bank, 1994a, Chapter 4)).

Severe financial repression (that is, large negative real interest rates) is bad for growth and should be removed quickly, taking account of the potential fis-

---

[123] See World Bank (1991), Chapter 5.

[124] Edwards (1989) provides a succinct discussion of these issues.

[125] Easterly (1992) presents an endogenous growth model that illustrates how different magnitudes of distortions can affect growth.

---

[126] Empirical studies investigating the links between trade liberalization and growth are summarized in *Kirmani*, Appendix I.

[127] Papageorgiou and others (1990) reach the same conclusion.

cal consequences *(WEO)*. The evidence on the effects of moderate financial repression, provided real interest rates on deposits are positive, is less clearcut. Holding interest rates slightly below market levels, along with bureaucratic direction of credit, may have had some beneficial effects on investment rates in some of the high-performing Asian economies (for example, Korea and Taiwan Province of China); however, it is doubtful whether the conditions for such a beneficial effect can be reproduced in most developing countries *(East Asia)*. In many low-income countries, effective implementation of prudential regulations seems to have been a particular problem, and progress in addressing the problems of troubled financial institutions was especially slow. A general lesson seems to be that broad financial reform needs to be accompanied by changes in the public enterprise sector and by a strengthening of the legal framework to enforce financial discipline. For example, bank recapitalizations in Africa—without a corresponding restructuring of public sector enterprises—have generally failed, with new balance sheet problems quickly re-emerging *(Africa* (World Bank, 1994a, Chapter 4)).

The experience of sub-Saharan Africa suggests that improvements in macroeconomic policy are not, by themselves, sufficient to trigger a substantial supply response from agriculture. However, when accompanied by other, micro-level reforms—most notably marketing board reforms—that raised real producer prices, the countries involved have typically achieved higher agricultural growth *(Africa* (World Bank, 1994a, Chapters 4 and 5)).[128]

Labor market data is extremely weak in many developing countries so it is often not possible to make definitive statements about the effects of adjustment policies; in many countries, the major form of quantity adjustment in the labor market has been a shift from formal to informal sector employment. Moreover, labor market reforms have typically been the most difficult of all to implement. Labor market rigidities—notably a slow responsiveness of real wages to labor market conditions—were prevalent in many countries with IMF-supported programs, but were addressed to only limited degrees *(CR)*. However, for those countries where relevant data is available, obtaining an initial decline in real wages at the outset of an adjustment effort appears to have helped to achieve macroeconomic adjustment without major unemployment *(Corbo)*. De facto or explicit arrangements for backward-looking indexation were especially problematic *(CR, Bruno)*.

---

[128] See also Krueger and others (1991).

Appendix II   Results from Cross-Country Growth Regressions

There is a large and growing body of empirical literature on factors influencing economic growth in the long term.[129] In this appendix, evidence drawn from a cross-country empirical analysis of long-term growth is used to examine, in turn, the following three questions:

• What does evidence from a broad panel of countries say about the correlation of particular policy-related variables with growth, capital accumulation, and productivity?

• What is the influence of factor accumulation and technological convergence on long-term growth?

• Taking into account the estimated influence of these long-term determinants of growth, how did the pattern of growth in the eight countries change over the different adjustment periods and how much of these changes can be explained by quantifiable policy-related variables?

Correlations Between Growth and Policy-Related Variables

To address the first question, a growth-accounting framework was used to assess empirically the links between policies and growth for as broad a group of countries as possible. One can then examine how these policy-related factors have fared in the eight countries. Annual real GDP growth, the rate of growth of the real capital stock, and the rate of growth of total factor productivity (TFP) are each regressed on a set of policy-related variables using pooled cross-section and time-series (panel) data for 92 industrial and developing countries over the period 1970–92.[130]

The evidence (Table 15) suggests that macroeconomic instability (as measured by inflation, fiscal deficits, and the black market exchange rate premium) is significantly negatively correlated with growth and that the links operate by dampening both capital accumulation and productivity—although causality is likely to run in both directions since adverse supply shocks are likely to raise inflation and put upward pressure on fiscal deficits.[131] Specifically, high inflation is associated with lower output and TFP growth and with slower capital accumulation. Fiscal surpluses are positively correlated with growth in output and TFP but are negatively correlated with capital accumulation. An examination of the separate influences of government saving and capital expenditure reveals that both are positively correlated with capital accumulation but that the coefficient on capital expenditures is larger than that on government saving. This finding suggests that government capital spending appears to increase overall capital accumulation (that is, private investment is not crowded out one-for-one). Large parallel market exchange rate premiums are negatively correlated with growth. Structural distortions—namely, high trade taxes and an underdeveloped financial system—and low educational attainment are also negatively correlated with growth; the effects appear to operate through both productivity gains and capital accumulation.[132] Finally, favorable terms of trade movements are found to be associated with higher growth, with the link operating mainly through their impact on productivity.

---

[129]Influential papers include those by Kormendi and Meguire (1985), Barro (1989), Mankiw, Romer, and Weil (1992), and Fischer (1993).

[130]The approach follows Fischer (1993). TFP is derived by subtracting the contributions of capital and labor accumulation from real GDP growth, assuming factor shares of 0.4 and 0.6 for capital and labor, respectively. Various alternative measures of TFP growth were all highly positively correlated.

[131]Given the inherent difficulty of constructing simple measures of policy variables, it is necessary to use proxies that will also be affected by non-policy-related factors. The exercise therefore should not be interpreted as a structural equation explaining growth. Also, the proportion of the variation in growth accounted for by such a regression is quite low—adjusted R^2s are typically in the range of 0.1 to 0.3.

[132]The difficulty of deriving simple measures to summarize the complex nature of structural distortions and reforms implies that it is often not possible to identify statistically robust relationships between growth and structural policies. The estimated partial correlations are typically highly sensitive to the proxies used, as well as to the coverage of countries and time periods. See Levine and Renelt (1992). However, microeconomic evidence based on ex-post rates of return on projects supported by the World Bank also suggests that trade distortions dampen the efficiency of investment. See World Bank (1991).

Table 15. Correlation Between Growth and Economic Policies, 1970–92[1]
(Period average, in percent unless otherwise indicated)

	Estimated Correlation with Growth	Estimated Correlation with Capital Accumulation	Estimated Correlation with TFP Growth	World	Developing Countries	Bangladesh	Chile	Ghana	India	Mexico	Morocco	Senegal	Thailand
Macroeconomic policies													
Inflation	– –	– –	– –	22	27	11	90	41	9	41	8	7	7
Budget surplus/GDP[3]	+	– –	++	-4.3	-4.3	-7.2	0.3	-4.0	-6.3	-6.3	-7.5	-2.8	-2.6
Capital expenditures/GDP[3]	+++	+++	…	4.7	5.7	…	2.7	2.8	1.9	4.1	9.4	3.5	3.6
Government savings/GDP[3]	+++	+++	++	0.5	1.3	…	3.0	–1.1	-4.4	-2.2	2.0	0.7	1.1
Exchange rate premium	– –	– – –	…	75	102	121	54	417	20	8	6	2	– –
External conditions													
Change in the terms of trade	+++	…	+++	-0.4	-0.5	1.0	-3.4	-2.7	0.9	-0.2	0.4	-0.3	-1.8
Structural policies													
Primary school enrollment rate	+++	…	++	85	78	61	100	61	72	100	52	43	81
Ratio of broad money to GDP	…	++	…	39	32	25	30	19	36	24	43	25	47
Average effective trade taxes[4]	…	– –	…	13	14	12	16	18	25	10	10	14	8

Source: IMF staff estimates.

[1]The partial correlations are estimated from three panel regressions (across country and time, with individual annual observations) for a large group of countries with growth in real GDP, capital accumulation, and TFP as dependent variables. TFP residuals are calculated as follows: TFP = ZGDP – 0.4 ZKAP – 0.6 ZLAB, where ZGDP is the rate of growth of real GDP, ZKAP is the rate of growth in the real capital stock, and ZLAB is the growth rate of the labor force. The data for ZGDP and GDP in 1970 are measured at PPP prices and are taken from the Penn World Tables, Mark 5.6; data for ZKAP are derived using data from the Penn World Tables, Mark 5.6, and the methodology proposed by King and Levine (1994); data for the budget surplus, government capital expenditure and saving, and the average effective import tax rate are from International Monetary Fund, Government Finance Statistics Yearbook, or staff country reports; data for inflation and broad money are from International Monetary Fund, International Financial Statistics; and all other variables are from Fischer (1993). +++ and – – – mean that the correlations are significant at the 1 percent level, and ++(– –) and +(–) imply significance at the 5 percent and 10 percent levels, respectively.

[2]World and developing country averages for inflation exclude Argentina, Bolivia, Brazil, and Nicaragua.

[3]The effects of the budget surplus, on the one hand, and capital expenditures and government saving, on the other, were estimated in separate panel regressions. The estimated effects of the other macroeconomic variables did not differ significantly between the two regressions.

[4]Measured as total trade taxes divided by the total value of merchandise trade.

To illustrate how these various factors may have affected long-term growth in the eight countries, Table 15 also presents period averages of the various policy-related variables. Important points to note are, first, Chile, Mexico, and Ghana experienced much higher rates of inflation than the other countries in the study; Ghana as well as Bangladesh also had larger exchange market distortions. In contrast, Morocco, Senegal, Thailand, and India had relatively stable macroeconomic environments (although significant exchange market distortions existed in India). Second, Bangladesh, Ghana, Morocco, Senegal, and, to some extent, India, began with markedly lower human capital endowments, measured by primary school enrollment rates. For these countries, fiscal adjustment that involved squeezing spending on primary education could be expected to be especially harmful to growth. Third, Ghana and India had distinctively more restrictive trade regimes, and Bangladesh and Ghana more underdeveloped financial sectors—although substantial structural changes took place in each of these countries over the period. Fourth, Chile, Ghana, and Thailand experienced the most unfavorable terms of trade movements on average during this period.

Long-Term Cross-Country Comparisons

The second question posed above is examined using cross-section regressions that link per capita real income growth to the accumulation of physical and human capital. Following Barro (1989), and based on a sample of 103 countries and data averaged over the period 1960 to 1992, per capita income growth is regressed on the share of investment in GDP, the growth rate of population, and measures of educational attainment as proxies for the accumulation of physical capital, labor, and human capital, respectively.[133] An additional explanatory variable is the relative income gap of each country with the United States in 1960—a term that is meant to capture the prediction of growth models that less technologically advanced economies would tend to catch up with more advanced ones.[134] The estimated parameters are then used to conduct a simple decomposition of growth into the part accounted for by factor accumulation and that due to productivity changes other than those arising from technological convergence. The results for the eight countries in this study are shown in Table 16.

The results suggest that the two most important variables contributing to growth are investment in physical capital and the achievement of basic levels of educational attainment, as measured by primary school enrollment rates. Population growth was found to have an insignificant impact on per capita growth. However, like other studies of this type, which generally find that factor accumulation accounts, on average, for between one half and two thirds of long-run growth, the right-hand-side variables explain only part of the differentials in long-term per capita growth. This suggests that, to varying degrees, long-term growth performance is also attributable to other influences, which include productivity developments not related to "catching up" and changes in the quality of factor inputs—both of which are influenced by economic policies.

After taking account of factor accumulation and technical convergence, actual growth is found to be higher than "predicted" growth, for five of the eight countries—Bangladesh, Mexico, Morocco, Senegal, and, most notably, Thailand. In Chile, Ghana, and, to a smaller extent, India, however, predicted growth is found to be higher than actual growth, suggesting that other influences, including policies, have tended to dampen productivity and growth, at least on average during this 30-year period.[135] However, it will be

---

[133]For the purposes of international comparison, growth rates for this exercise are measured at purchasing power parity (PPP) adjusted prices. For most of the eight countries, it does not make much difference whether growth is measured at national or international relative prices. However, for a few countries, there do appear to be sizable differences during selected periods. The differences are often most marked in periods when the trade and exchange system was especially distorted (for example, Bangladesh during 1970–79) because growth is weighted in favor of protected sectors that benefit from high domestic relative prices, or during periods following substantial exchange or trade reforms (for example, Ghana after 1983 and Mexico in 1988–92) as sectors with a comparative advantage expand more rapidly. Since growth at national prices directly affects welfare and is how the effects of policies are usually assessed, it is the measure used for the panel estimates discussed later in this appendix.

[134]This specification, which follows Barro (1989) and the World Bank (1993b), is generally associated with tests of theories of endogenous growth, which are generally predicated on the assumption that "knowledge" and factor accumulation interact to produce increasing returns to scale. Therefore, an economy can be on various possible long-run growth paths, depending upon the level of investment and activity in areas that benefit most from such factors. However, it is also consistent with the transitional dynamics of a neoclassical growth model that incorporates human capital. The results should be interpreted with caution, however, as the estimated equation explains less than one half of the variation in per capita income growth. Moreover, the approach requires the assumption that all countries have the same production function. The quality of the data for several countries is also poor, and it is impossible to identify the direction of biases so introduced.

[135]Because of the severe depth of the 1975 and 1983 recessions in Chile, growth rates in subsequent years were heavily influenced by changes in the degree of capacity utilization. However, such factors would be less likely to influence long-term average growth.

Table 16. Determinants of Per Capita Income Growth, 1960–92
(Dependent variable: average annual per capita real GDP growth)

	Parameter Estimate	Bangladesh Sample mean	Contribution	Chile Sample mean	Contribution	Ghana Sample mean	Contribution	India Sample mean	Contribution
CONSTANT	−0.07		−0.07		−0.07		−0.07		−0.07
INV	0.13	4.1	0.52	20.0	2.56	6.0	0.76	13.8	1.76
POPG	−0.19	2.4	−0.46	1.8	−0.34	2.6	−0.50	2.2	−0.42
GAP60	−3.77	0.1	−0.36	0.3	−1.10	0.1	−0.34	0.1	−0.29
PRIM60	1.23	0.5	0.58	1.1	1.34	0.6	0.72	0.6	0.75
SEC60	0.74	0.1	0.06	0.2	0.18	—	0.02	0.2	0.15
Estimated total			0.26		2.57		0.60		1.88
Actual			1.44		1.65		0.21		1.61
Actual as a percentage of estimated			550		64		35		86

	Parameter Estimate	Mexico Sample mean	Contribution	Morocco Sample mean	Contribution	Senegal Sample mean	Contribution	Thailand Sample mean	Contribution
CONSTANT	−0.07		−0.07		−0.07		−0.07		−0.07
INV	0.13	16.5	2.11	9.1	1.16	5.0	0.64	18.4	2.35
POPG	−0.19	2.5	−0.47	2.5	−0.47	2.5	−0.48	2.5	−0.47
GAP60	−3.77	0.3	−1.08	0.1	−0.31	0.1	−0.40	0.1	−0.36
PRIM60	1.23	0.8	0.98	0.5	0.58	0.3	0.33	0.8	1.02
SEC60	0.74	0.1	0.08	0.1	0.04	—	0.02	0.1	0.09
Estimated total			1.55		0.93		0.05		2.56
Actual			2.47		3.06		0.22		4.47
Actual as a percentage of estimated			159		331		428		175

Source: IMF staff estimates.

Note: The estimated equation is $GRTH = -0.069 + 0.128\ INV^{***} - 0.190\ POPG + 1.228\ PRI60^{**} + 0.742\ SEC60 - 3.771\ GAP60^{***}$
$$(-0.12) \quad (4.40) \quad\quad (-1.18) \quad\quad (2.09) \quad\quad (0.72) \quad\quad (-3.58),$$
Adjusted $R^2 = 0.45$
Number of countries: 103

where *GRTH* stands for per capita GDP growth; *INV* refers to the ratio of investment to GDP; and *GAP60* is the ratio of country *i* income to that of the United States in 1960, all measured at international (PPP) prices. *POPG* is the growth rate of the population, *PRI60* and *SEC60* refer to primary and secondary school enrollment rates, respectively. Data for *GRTH, INV, GAP60,* and *POPG* are taken from the Penn World Tables, Mark 5.6, and *PRIM60* and *SEC60* are from the World Bank's World Tables. Heteroskedastic-consistent *t*-statistics are in parentheses. *** and ** imply significance at the 1 percent and 5 percent levels, respectively.

shown in the next section that these period averages mask important shifts over time.

Performance During Different Adjustment Periods

Changes in growth performance in the eight countries during different phases of adjustment can be considered on the basis of the cross-country regressions of the long-term determinants of growth. Specifically, the following questions are examined:

• Was growth in the eight countries—after taking into account the long-term determinants of growth discussed above—significantly below or above the "world average" before, during, and after adjustment?

• Do the policy-related factors discussed earlier explain most of these growth differentials and how they have shifted over the different adjustment periods?

Following an approach suggested by Bruno and Easterly (1995), the regression discussed above is re-estimated with the following modifications: for each country under consideration, the 1970–92 period is divided into three (or four) subperiods corresponding to the identified adjustment phases and data are averaged over these subperiods.[136] A panel regression is then estimated across these subperiods and over the whole sample of countries (totaling 92) with two sets of dummy variables—one for each subperiod for all countries and one for each subperiod for the country of interest.[137] The coefficients on the individual country dummies are reported in Table 17 (growth differential A) and in Chart 10. These "growth differentials" can be interpreted as the extent to which each country's growth in each subperiod differed from the world average after controlling for the long-run determinants of growth and exogenous shocks common to the growth experience of all countries.

On the basis of this exercise, the eight countries can be classified into several groups according to the growth response over the different adjustment periods:

• Chile, Ghana, and Mexico paid a substantial price, in terms of negative growth differentials, during the first phase of their adjustment. Chile and

Ghana, however, achieved a large and sustained turnaround associated with a large positive growth differential later in the adjustment process; the length of the recovery in Chile especially, spanning more than a decade, suggests more than a reversion-to-trend phenomenon. In contrast, the revival in Mexico was much more muted; the growth differential during the second adjustment phase (1988–93), while positive, was relatively small. This suggests that, unlike most other countries (including Chile and Ghana) that achieved substantial reductions in inflation, Mexico did not benefit from a large post-stabilization rebound in per capita growth relative to the world average.

• Bangladesh shifted from a situation where growth was markedly below the world average prior to adjustment to positive growth differentials in the respective adjustment periods.

• In Morocco, Senegal, and India, no sustained shift in growth differentials occurred between the preadjustment and adjustment periods.[138] Unlike the other two countries, however, Morocco's growth performance remained above the world average in all periods, despite major adverse supply shocks.

• Thailand stands out with much stronger growth relative to the world average throughout the period. No decline in the growth differential was observed during the adjustment period, and the post-adjustment growth differential widened markedly.

A second set of growth differentials (line B in Table 17) was estimated by adding to the right-hand side a set of policy-related variables (inflation, the budget deficit, and the parallel market exchange premium).[139] This specification provides an alternative approach to measuring growth differentials in which the role of macroeconomic policies is explicitly taken into account.[140]

An important conclusion from this exercise is that the quantifiable proxies for macroeconomic policies do have additional explanatory power in periods when countries experienced episodes of massive macroeconomic instability (for example, high infla-

---

[136]As noted earlier, the subperiods chosen here do not necessarily correspond to the timing of IMF-supported programs.

[137]The constant is omitted from the regression and the change in the terms of trade is added to the list of right-hand-side variables. The inclusion of a broad group of other countries in the regression helps to control for other exogenous influences common to all countries (for example, changes in world economic conditions), but does not correct for country-specific reversion-to-trend effects.

[138]Senegal's rather variable growth performance appears to be largely the result of the impact of supply shocks. See Tahari and others (forthcoming).

[139]It was not possible to include variables proxying structural policies in this part of the exercise because the available measures were typically computed as period averages or at a limited number of points in time over the sample period. It should also be recognized that the interpretation of this policy-augmented growth regression is not straightforward, as policies also affect investment, which is included as a regressor; one possible interpretation of the coefficients on the policy variables in this regression is that they capture, broadly speaking, the influence of policies on productivity.

[140]Since the differentials A and B are derived from different specifications of the growth equation, a direct comparison of the two is not possible.

Table 17. Estimates of Per Capita Growth Differentials
After Controlling for Long-Run Determinants of Growth and Some Policy Factors[1]
(Average annual growth differential, in percentage points)

	Preadjustment Period	First Adjustment Period	Second Adjustment Period	Postadjustment Period	Adjusted R[2] of the Associated Regression
Bangladesh[2]	1970–80	1981–84	1985–92		
A. Growth differential after controlling for all long-run determinants and changes in the terms of trade	−4.2*** (7.0)	2.5*** (6.2)	2.9*** (9.6)	...	0.37
B. Growth differential after controlling for long-run determinants, terms of trade changes, and policies	−3.8*** (6.6)	2.1*** (4.5)	2.3*** (6.4)	...	0.43
Chile	1970–73	1974–83	1984–89	1990–93	
A. Growth differential after controlling for all long-run determinants and changes in the terms of trade	−3.6*** (7.3)	−1.0 (1.1)	3.0*** (7.6)	3.1*** (9.3)	0.31
B. Growth differential after controlling for long-run determinants, terms of trade changes, and policies	−1.9** (2.9)	−1.2 (−1.1)	2.4*** (5.2)	2.8*** (7.7)	0.39
Ghana	1970–82	1983–86	1987–91	1992–93	
A. Growth differential after controlling for all long-run determinants and changes in the terms of trade	−2.4*** (7.7)	1.3*** (3.0)	2.7*** (6.6)	2.3*** (4.3)	0.25
B. Growth differential after controlling for long-run determinants, terms of trade changes, and policies	−1.8*** (3.1)	1.7** (2.8)	2.1*** (3.8)	...	0.36
India[2]	1970–90	1991–93			
A. Growth differential after controlling for all long-run determinants and changes in the terms of trade	0.5 (0.9)	−0.6 (0.8)	...	...	0.21
B. Growth differential after controlling for long-run determinants, terms of trade changes, and policies	0.5 (0.9)	−0.3 (0.3)	...	...	0.34
Mexico	1970–82	1983–87	1988–93		
A. Growth differential after controlling for all long-run determinants and changes in the terms of trade	2.1*** (7.3)	−1.4*** (3.7)	0.5 (1.4)	...	0.31

Table 17 (concluded)

	Preadjustment Period	First Adjustment Period	Second Adjustment Period	Postadjustment Period	Adjusted R^2 of the Associated Regression
B. Growth differential after controlling for long-run determinants, terms of trade changes, and policies	2.2*** (7.4)	−0.6 (1.2)	0.3 (0.8)	...	0.39
Morocco	*1970–80*	*1981–85*	*1986–93*		
A. Growth differential after controlling for all long-run determinants and changes in the terms of trade	1.2*** (4.0)	1.5*** (4.5)	0.9*** (3.1)	...	0.34
B. Growth differential after controlling for long-run determinants, terms of trade changes, and policies	1.0*** (3.1)	1.2*** (3.5)	0.4 (1.3)	...	0.44
Senegal	*1970–84*	*1985–88*	*1989–93*		
A. Growth differential after controlling for all long-run determinants and changes in the terms of trade	— (—)	1.9*** (5.8)	−0.8** (2.1)	...	0.30
B. Growth differential after controlling for long-run determinants, terms of trade changes, and policies	−0.4 (1.3)	1.1** (2.9)	−1.5*** (3.5)	...	0.41
Thailand	*1970–80*	*1981–86*	*1987–93*		
A. Growth differential after controlling for all long-run determinants and changes in the terms of trade	2.1*** (9.1)	2.9*** (10.1)	6.8*** (16.1)	...	0.36
B. Growth differential after controlling for long-run determinants, terms of trade changes, and policies	2.1*** (8.6)	2.7*** (8.3)	6.4*** (12.8)	...	0.43

Source: IMF staff estimates.

[1]Following an approach suggested by Bruno and Easterly (1995), the growth differentials are defined as the estimated coefficients on the dummy variables for each country (that is, the estimated ß's) in Barro-style growth regressions using pooled data on the average growth rates over the respective subperiods and across 92 countries. The estimated equations took the following form:

$$GRTH_{it} = \sum_{t=1}^{T} \gamma_t DUM_{it} + \sum_{t=1}^{T} \beta_t DUMI_t + \alpha_1 INV + \alpha_2 POPG + \alpha_3 GAP70 + \alpha_4 PRI70 + \alpha_5 SEC70 + \alpha_6 \Delta TOT$$

In addition, the following policy-related factors were added to the regressors underlying the second set of results reported for each country:

$$\alpha_7 INFL + \alpha_8 BUDSUP + \alpha_9 PREMIUM + \alpha_{10} HINFL,$$

where T is the number of subperiods in each case; $GRTH$ is the growth rate of real per capita GDP measured in terms of constant domestic prices; INV is the share of investment in GDP; $POPG$ is the growth rate of the population; $GAP70$ is the ratio of country i income to that of the United States in 1970; $PRI70$ and $SEC70$ are primary and secondary school enrollment rates, respectively, in 1970; $INFL$ is the average annual rate of inflation in the CPI; $BUDSUP$ is the government budgetary surplus as a percent of GDP; $PREMIUM$ is the average premium between the parallel market and official market exchange rates; and ΔTOT is the change in the ratio of export prices to import prices. Data for $GRTH$ are taken from Bruno and Easterly (1995). Data for all other variables are from the same sources as listed in Tables 15 and 16. Possible nonlinearities in the effects of inflation on growth are taken account of by including the variable $HINFL$, which takes the value of the inflation rate when it is greater than 40 percent. $DUMi$ are the dummies for each period for all countries and $DUMI$ are dummies for the country being examined, one for each period. Absolute values of heteroskedastic-consistent t-statistics are in parentheses. *** denotes significance at the 1 percent level, and ** and * at the 5 percent and 10 percent levels, respectively.

[2]Fiscal year data.

tion or extreme distortions in the exchange market): Chile in the early 1970s, Ghana prior to the adoption of the Economic Recovery Program, and Mexico after the debt crisis. Although there are always problems of establishing the direction of causation, since exogenous factors that lower output may also put upward pressure on inflation, the results suggest that early action to prevent such episodes is likely to be beneficial to growth.

For countries that experienced long periods of macroeconomic stability, most notably Thailand, the proxies for macroeconomic policies tend to have less significant explanatory power, suggesting that an important part of the variation in growth in some of these countries (notably Thailand) is due to factors (including confidence effects) other than those captured by the macroeconomic policy variables included here.

Appendix III   Medium-Term Fiscal Sustainability and Its Consistency with Low Inflation

Assessments of the sustainability and internal consistency of policies by the private sector can greatly influence the response of private investment. An important consideration in any such assessment is how the stance of fiscal policy will affect the public sector debt burden. A path of primary fiscal balances that implied either continued large increases in the ratio of public debt to GDP or continued heavy use of the inflation tax would be less credible. As an indication of the progress made toward fiscal sustainability in each of the eight countries, Chart 23 presents the results of some debt dynamics, based on the intertemporal budget constraint for the public sector.

The actual primary fiscal balance is compared with two notions of a "sustainable" balance: (1) the primary balance that would keep the public debt-to-GDP ratio constant on the assumption that the current rate of inflation (and hence seigniorage) and the current interest rate on domestic debt (and hence the magnitude of financial repression) are maintained in the future; and (2) the primary balance that would keep the public debt-to-GDP ratio constant in a context of low inflation and no financial repression.[141] This latter measure is a more comprehensive indicator of fiscal sustainability, since it provides a measure of the deficit reduction that is needed to make fiscal policy consistent with other important goals of an adjustment strategy, namely low inflation and efficient financial intermediation.

Judged by the above criteria, a significant move toward a more sustainable fiscal stance occurred in all eight countries. In the "preadjustment" period, the actual primary deficit was much higher than the sustainable balance in most countries (Bangladesh, India, Mexico, Morocco, and Senegal).[142] During the adjustment periods, the actual primary balance was sharply reduced in all countries, and in some (Mexico, Morocco, and Thailand) shifted to a level that significantly exceeded either of the two indicators of a sustainable balance.[143] Moreover, financial repression was an important feature of the preadjustment or early adjustment periods in Chile, Ghana, India, Mexico, and Morocco. The substantial convergence in the two sustainability criteria over time indicates the reduced reliance on the inflation tax and on financial repression as means of financing the budget deficits.

One would thus conclude that fiscal adjustments had moved the path of public debt to well within the sustainable range, in the narrow sense used here, in Chile, Mexico, Morocco, and Thailand. A similar unambiguous conclusion is difficult in the cases of Bangladesh, Ghana, India, and Senegal. However, external borrowing on concessional terms is important in these countries, and has contributed to keeping the effective real interest rate on public debt at or below the rate of growth of real GDP. In these circumstances, there is no long-term solvency con-

---

[141]The intertemporal budget constraint for the public sector can be described as $\dot{b} = (r - n)\,b + d - s$ where b, d, and s represent public debt, the primary deficit, and seigniorage revenues (including the inflation tax), respectively (all as shares of GDP), r represents the average real interest rate on debt, and n is the real GDP growth rate (see Anand and van Wijnbergen (1989)). The aim is to assess whether fiscal policy was sustainable *at the time*, rather than with the benefit of hindsight. Consequently, the calculations are based on a three-year moving average of actual values of interest rates and growth rates and assume that the real exchange rate is expected to be constant. The estimate of "low-inflation" seigniorage used in the calculations was derived from a quadratic function linking seigniorage to inflation that was estimated by Easterly and others (1994) on the basis of cross-country data and assuming an annual inflation rate of 5 percent. This measure may underestimate the potential for noninflationary seigniorage in countries such as India, where currency holdings are relatively large.

[142]The sustainability calculations for Bangladesh are based on external debt, because of the paucity of data on domestic debt. However, rough estimates of the size of domestic public debt (at about 10 percent of GDP) suggest that its inclusion would not fundamentally alter the results.

[143] In Chile, fiscal sustainability has not really been an issue except in 1982–85, when domestic public debt increased sharply as a result of recapitalization of the banking system. A similar point applies to Bangladesh, where there have been several bank recapitalizations in recent years.

Chart 23. Actual and Sustainable Primary Fiscal Balances[1]
(In percent of GDP)

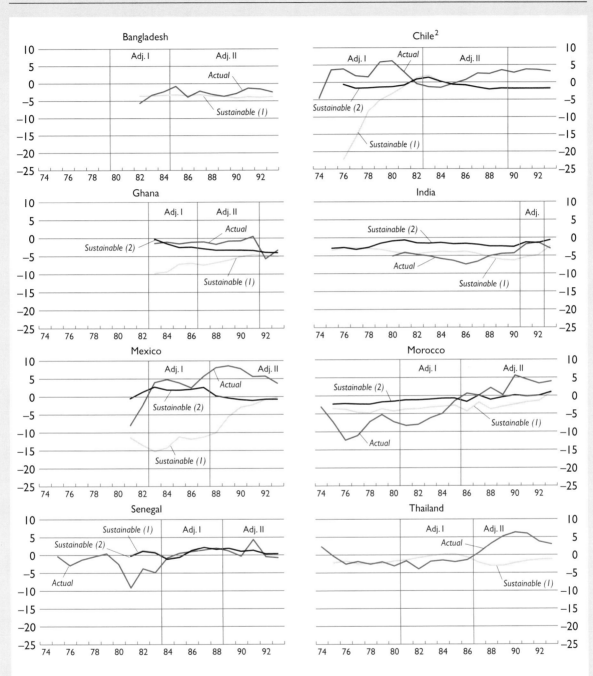

Sources: World Bank, World Debt Tables; and IMF staff estimates.

[1] Primary balance includes grants. Sustainable (1) is the balance consistent with constant public-to-debt ratio. Sustainable (2) is the balance consistent with constant public-to-debt ratio, low inflation and no financial repression.

[2] Primary balance for Chile includes quasi-fiscal losses of the central bank.

straint in the sense that the debt-to-GDP ratio will not grow without bounds.[144]

Of course, the measures of fiscal sustainability are partial in that they focus only on the capacity to service and repay outstanding debt. They do not address the more fundamental issue of whether a fiscal balance is also consistent with other macroeconomic objectives, including for the external current account balance. In this latter respect, the fiscal policy responses to recent capital inflows have differed substantially, with potentially important consequences for growth (see Section VII). Moreover, the permanence of fiscal measures used to obtain a sustainable balance can also be a major issue.

---

[144] In 1993, the shares of external debt on concessional terms in total external debt were Bangladesh, 98 percent; Ghana, 83 percent; India, 53 percent; and Senegal, 70 percent. If all concessional lending were to be phased out and replaced by borrowing at market terms, then, based on the 1993 debt composition, interest payments would increase as follows: Bangladesh, 1.6 percentage points of GDP; Ghana, 1.4 percentage points; India, 0.5 percentage point; and Senegal, 2 percentage points.

Appendix IV   Econometric Evidence on the Determinants of Private Investment

The econometric analysis of private investment in the eight countries was guided by two considerations. First, all the time series were expressed either in scaled form or in rates of change to ensure stationarity and avoid spurious correlation.[145] Second, the preferred equations were derived from a specification search selecting a parsimonious model from a larger initial set of explanatory variables, by successively eliminating statistically insignificant or implausibly signed regressors.[146]

The investment equations were estimated by ordinary least squares, for two reasons. First, the full range of factors affecting investment cannot be captured quantitatively (for example, in the case of structural reforms and their impact on private sector expectations). This underscores the importance of selecting an estimation technique relatively robust to misspecification errors in small samples.[147] Nevertheless, to reduce the risks of simultaneity bias, the activity variable was specified with a one-period lag.[148] Second, unlike instrumental variable techniques, ordinary least squares are not affected by the problem of potential dependence of results on the choice of instruments. Recursive least squares were used to account for the possibility of time-varying parameters, given the potential for shifts in policy regimes and changes in the nature of exogenous shocks.

The results, summarized in Table 18 and discussed in the main text, confirm that estimated equations broadly conforming to standard specifications of investment functions for developing countries are able to account for most of the variation of private investment in each of the eight countries. The estimates generally underscore the important role of accelerator-type effects (except for Bangladesh), indicators of financial policies, and measures of uncertainty and macroeconomic stability in explaining the observed pattern of private investment.

---

[145]Low or rapidly decaying values of the sample autocorrelation function indicated that nonstationarity was in no instance a problem. The small sample size prevents a reliable use of formal unit root tests.

[146]This modeling strategy potentially minimizes omitted variable bias, although accuracy may be affected by highly collinear regressors. The general-to-specific approach faced inevitable degrees of freedom constraints in instances where only a small sample of observations was available.

---

[147] Available small sample studies show that when an estimated equation incorrectly omits relevant explanatory variables, ordinary least squares are less sensitive to misspecification than simultaneous estimation methods and therefore may be a preferable estimation technique. See Mariano (1982) and Phillips (1983).

[148] Standard errors were computed using White's heteroskedasticity-consistent variance-covariance estimator.

Table 18. Summary of Investment Equations[1]

Country	Sample (Number of annual observations)	Endogenous Variable (In percent of GDP)	Explanatory Variables:				
			Aggregate activity	Financial variables:		Public investment (In percent of GDP)	Foreign exchange availability
				Real interest rate/ user cost	Credit availability		
Bangladesh	1979/80–1993/94 (15 obs.)	Priv. inv. (constant prices, logs)	Not signif., omitted	VAR.: real lending rate k COEF: – – –	VAR.: real growth of private sector credit COEF:+	Not signif., omitted	VAR.: reserves in monthsof imports (logs) COEF: +++
Chile	1975–93 (19 obs.)	Nongovt. inv. (constant prices, logs)	VAR.: Real GDP growth, lagged COEF: +++	(Real lending rate not signif., omitted) VAR.: relative price inv./GDP COEF: – –	Not signif, omitted	VAR.: govt. inv. (constant prices, logs) COEF: – – –	Not signif, omitted
Ghana	1971–93 (23 obs.)	Priv. inv. (current prices, logs)	VAR.: real GDP growth, lagged COEF: +++	VAR.: real lending rate COEF: –	Not signif, omitted	VAR.: publ. inv. (current prices, lagged, logs) COEF: – – –	Not signif., omitted
India	1973/74–1993/94 (21 obs.)	Priv. inv. (constant prices, logs)	VAR.: Lagged growth of industrial production COEF:++	VAR.: real lending rate COEF: –	VAR.: real growth of private sector credit COEF: +	VAR.: publ. inv. (constant prices, logs) COEF: – – –	Not signif., omitted
Mexico	1972–93 (22 obs.)	Priv. inv. (current prices, logs)	VAR.: real GDP growth lagged COEF: +++	VAR.: real deposit rate COEF: –	VAR.: real growth of private sector credit COEF: ++	VAR.: publ. inv. (current prices, logs) COEF: – – –	Not signif., omitted
	1981–93 (13 obs.)	Priv. inv. (constant prices, logs)	VAR.: real GDP growth, lagged COEF: ++	VAR.: real deposit rate COEF: – – –	VAR.: real growth of private sector credit COEF: ++	VAR.: publ. inv. (constant prices, logs) COEF: –	
Morocco	1972–93 (22 obs.)	Priv. inv. (constant prices, logs)	VAR.: Real GDP growth, lagged COEF: +	VAR.: real 6-month T-bill rate COEF: – – –	VAR.: real growth of nongovt. sector credit COEF: +	VAR.: publ. inv. (constant prices, logs) COEF: +++	Not signif., omitted
Senegal	1978–93 (16 obs.)	Nongovt. inv. (constant prices, logs)	VAR.: Real GDP growth, lagged COEF: +	Not signif., omitted	Not signif, omitted	VAR.: govt. inv. (constant prices, logs) COEF: – –	
Thailand	1970–93 (24 obs.)	Priv. inv. (constant prices, logs)	VAR.: Real GDP growth in partner countries COEF: +++	VAR.: Real lending rate COEF: –	Omitted	VAR.: publ. inv. (constant prices, logs) COEF: – – –	Not signif., omitted

Explanatory Variables:

Country	Measures of uncertainty/macroeconomic instability			External shocks	Lagged dependent variable	Estimation Technique and Fit
	Inflation rate/ parallel market premium/REER	External debt/ debt service	Sample variable measures (or other)			
Bangladesh		VAR.: external debt service/exports (logs) COEF.: – – –	VAR.: variance REER COEF.: – – – (variance of inflation and real interest rate not signif., omitted)		COEF: +++	OLS-White HCSE $\bar{R}^2$ = 0.74 Durbin's h-statistic = –0.34
Chile	Not signif., omitted	VAR.: external debt service/exports (logs) COEF.: – – –	Not signif., omitted	Not signif., omitted	Not signif., omitted	OLS-White HCSE $\bar{R}^2$ = 0.81 DW statistic = 1.52
Ghana	VAR.: exchange rate premium (logs) COEF.: – – –	Not signif., omitted	(Variance of nominal exchange rate not signif., omitted)	VAR.: export price shock (in % of GDP) COEF.: ++	Not signif., omitted	OLS-White HCSE $\bar{R}^2$ = 0.76 DW statistic = 1.87
India	Not signif., omitted	Not signif., omitted	VAR.: Variance of WPI inflation rate. COEF.: – – – VAR.: Variance of real exchange rate changes COEF.: –		COEF: +++	OLS-White HCSE $\bar{R}^2$ = 0.66 Durbin's h-statistic = –1.82
Mexico	Not signif., omitted	Not signif., omitted	VAR.: variance of industrial production COEF.: –	Not signif., omitted	COEF: ++	OLS-White HCSE $\bar{R}^2$ = 0.63 Durbin's h-statistic = 0.62
	VAR.: CPI inflation rate COEF.: – – –		Variance of industrial production not signif., omitted		COEF: ++	OLS-White HCSE $\bar{R}^2$ = 0.84 Durbin's h-statistic = –0.47
Morocco	VAR.: REER level (logs) COEF.: – – –	Not signif., omitted	Variance of CPI inflation not signif., omitted	VAR.: export price shock (in % of GDP) COEF.: ++ VAR.: import price shock (in % of GDP) COEF.: –	COEF: +++	OLS-White HCSE $\bar{R}^2$ = 0.74 Durbin's h-statistic = –0.74
Senegal	VAR.: CPI inflation rate COEF.: – – – VAR.: REER level (logs) COEF.: – – –	VAR.: Ext. debt/ GDP (logs) COEF.: – –	VAR.: govt. domestic borrowing/GDP COEF.: –		Not signif., omitted	OLS-White HCSE $\bar{R}^2$ = 0.86 DW statistic = 2.71
Thailand	VAR.: RULC level (logs) COEF.: – – –	Not signif., omitted	Variance of inflation not signif., omitted	Not signif., omitted	COEF: +++	OLS-White HCSE $\bar{R}^2$ = 0.91 Durbin's h-statistic = –0.00

Source: IMF staff estimates.

[1] +, –: Sign of the coefficient, not statistically significant at 5 percent level, but significant at a marginally higher level.

++, – –: Sign of the coefficient, statistically significant at 5 percent.

+++, – – –: Sign of the coefficient, statistically significant at 1 percent.

Appendix V Trade and Financial Sector Reform and Labor Market Characteristics

This appendix presents background information referred to in Sections IV and VIII. The material is organized in three summary tables: trade reforms (Table 19), financial sector reform (Table 20), and labor market characteristics (Table 21).

Table 19. Main Elements of Trade Reforms

Country (Initial year of reforms)	Status Prior to Reforms	Major Reform Elements	Status in Mid-1995
Bangladesh (1985–86)	High tariffs and extensive use of quantitative restrictions (QRs); high degree of tariff escalation.	Initial sharp reduction in number of tariff bands. Gradual reduction in QRs. Significant progress was only made starting in 1991.	Despite reforms, system remains complex and contains many discretionary elements.
Chile (1974)	Severely distorted trade system, with average nominal tariff of 105 percent; high dispersion; extensive QRs; and multiple exchange rates.	Rapid replacement of QRs with tariffs; tariffs unified at 35 percent.	Simplified trade system in place with uniform tariff rate of 11 percent.
Ghana (1983)	Severely distorted trade system with highly overvalued exchange rate; virtually all imports covered by QRs; extensive taxation of cocoa exports.	Substantial reduction in QRs; maximum tariff reduced from 50 percent to an essentially uniform tariff of 30 percent. Cocoa taxation reduced. In 1986, uniform tariff replaced with four-tiered system with escalating structure to protect consumer goods and luxury items. Import surcharge levied in 1988 and super sales tax on luxury goods imports in 1990.	Despite some reversals, system is much less restrictive and complex than before reforms.
India (1991)	Severely restrictive and complex trade regime with proliferation of QRs and high and dispersed tariffs. Imports of consumer goods virtually banned.	Reforms began with removal of export restrictions and of QRs on intermediate and capital goods. Reductions in the level of dispersion of tariffs.	Average tariffs remain high and large share of domestic production—especially of consumer goods—still protected by QRs.
Mexico (1985)	Following debt crisis in 1982, many previously reduced trade restrictions reinstated. Widespread trade and exchange controls in use.	Preannounced program of reductions in coverage of QRs; extensive cuts during the first two years. Coverage of official reference prices reduced significantly. Preannounced schedule of planned tariff reductions; maximum tariff reduced in one step from 100 percent to 50 percent. Joined General Agreement on Tarriffs and Trade (GATT) in 1986.	Considerably more liberal, simplified, and outward-oriented trade regime. Remaining import licensing controls affect mainly agricultural and agroindustrial products, oil and derivatives, cars and trucks.
Morocco (1983)	Relatively high tariffs and widespread use of QRs. High discrimination against labor-intensive activities.	Early focus of trade reforms was sharp reduction in QRs and official reference prices. Maximum tariff reduced in one step from 400 percent to 60 percent with subsequent further reductions. In 1987, joined GATT and bound a large share of tariffs.	Although only a moderate reduction in average nominal tariffs, the system is much simpler and less distorted. Virtually all tariffs bound under the Uruguay Round.
Senegal (1986)	High tariff protection, widespread use of QRs, and selective trade and tax preferences.	Reform program began with the reduction of QRs and a moderate reduction in the maximum tariff rate. Reforms almost fully reversed three years later owing to revenue shortfalls. Average import taxes, which had declined from 98 percent in 1986 to 35 percent in 1988, were back up to 90 percent in 1992, and the use of official reference prices was broadened. In late 1994, the requirement of prior authorization for certain imports and exports was eliminated.	By 1992, Senegal's trade protection was no lower than before the start of reforms, and possibly was more complex. A new phase of reforms launched in 1994 has reduced the restrictiveness of the system.
Thailand	Relatively low levels of protection. Trade regime relatively outward oriented but significant intervention through selective tax preferences. Coverage of QRs very low. Protection biased against agriculture and toward capital-intensive import substituting industries.	Only minor initial tariff reductions with some reversal owing partly to fiscal constraints. Export taxation, especially of rice, eliminated in 1986. Tariff reduction on 4,000 product lines in 1995; average tariff to be reduced to 17 percent by 1997.	Trade system remains relatively unchanged with average nominal tariffs at about 30 percent and a relatively large number of tariff rates.

Table 20. Main Elements of Financial Sector Reforms

Country (Initial year of reforms)	Status of Financial Sector Prior to Reform	Key Elements of Reforms	Important Outcomes
Bangladesh (late 1980s)	Small and relatively underdeveloped financial sector dominated by commercial banks. Complex structure of interest rates subject to controls. Extensive quantitative credit controls. Growing share of nonperforming loans. Weak supervisory framework.	Significant progress with liberalizing interest rates. Some steps to strengthen prudential regulations.	Real interest rates positive though not market determined. Spreads remain high, reflecting lack of competition, defaults, and nonperforming loans. Some evidence of financial deepening, but an insignificant increase in private sector's share of total credit; other aspects of financial system remain relatively underdeveloped.
Chile (1974 and 1981)	Prior to 1974, domestic financial system was fully publicly owned and heavily regulated through interest rate ceilings, quantitative controls on banks, substantial directed credit, and restrictions on operations of financial institutions. Real interest rates were negative.	Privatization and restructuring of the banking system; interest rates liberalized; quantitative credit controls abolished. However, weaknesses in bank supervision and prudential regulations as well as excessive deregulation led to a massive accumulation of nonperforming loans, which were further fueled by speculative capital inflows in the late 1970s. This was followed by a series of bank failures. Major reforms of supervisory and regulatory framework in 1982–83.	Initial sharp increase in real interest rates that did not narrow until mid-1980s. Financial crisis in early 1980s. Significant financial deepening, measured by the share of broad money, plus other financial assets to GDP and in private sector's share of domestic credit.
Ghana (1988)	Underdeveloped and heavily regulated financial sector. Controls on interest rates led to highly negative real rates; together with pre-emption of financial resources by Government, this led to severe financial repression and inefficiencies in banking system.	Controls on deposit and lending rates and on credit lifted starting in 1988. Institutional reforms of the banking system implemented in 1989–90. Government took over large part of nonperforming portfolios of commercial banks.	Real interest rates turned positive in 1991 (lending rates) and 1992 (deposit rates). Spread between deposit and lending rates widened. No significant change in the ratio of M2 to GDP; moderate increase in the private sector's share of total credit.
India (1991)	Highly regulated and inefficient financial markets with controls on interest rates, quantitative credit allocation, government-owned banking system, and public sector pre-emption of a large proportion of financial resources.	Interest rate structure simplified and rates adjusted. In 1994, lending rates liberalized. Government pre-emptions reduced by lowering reserve requirements and remunerating bank holdings of government securities at market-determined rates. Some reduction in directed credit and prudential regulations strengthened. Substantial liberalization of broader financial system, but banking system remains dominated by government-owned banks.	Since late 1994, when interest rates were liberalized, spreads have narrowed but remain high reflecting the lack of competition and high inter-mediation costs. Financial deepening, especially if measured by a broader financial aggregate, occurred, although private sector's share of total credit remained broadly unchanged. Some reduction in the share of bank credit to priority sectors.

Country			
Mexico (1988–89)	Until the mid-1970s, ceilings on interest rates and extensive use of directed credit. But inflation was low during this period. Capital flight in late 1970s weakened banking system. In 1982 commercial banks were nationalized and there was a forced conversion of foreign exchange-denominated deposits at non-market rates.	In late 1988, financial sector reform program launched consisting of interest rate decontrol; rationalization of reserve requirements; and removal of mandatory subsidized lending to the public sector and restriction on lending to the private sector. Banks reprivatized in 1991-92.	Period of financial disintermediation between 1982–88. Capital inflows that began in late 1980s led to expansion in bank balance sheets. Increasing ratio of nonperforming bank loans since 1988 associated with insufficient ability to assess credit risk. Limits imposed in 1992 on banks' open foreign exchange position and exposure to exchange risk.
Morocco (1985)	Heavily regulated financial sector. Quantitative credit controls. Interest rate controls resulted in significantly negative real interest rates in 1980s.	Interest rates liberalized gradually. Credit ceilings abolished in early 1991. New banking law adopted in 1993 to strengthen bank supervisory framework.	Interest rates are positive but not market determined. Government retains preferential access to financial resources, resulting in high taxation of financial intermediation. Indicators of financial sector development show moderate progress.
Senegal (1988)	Regulated financial sector, almost fully publicly owned. Quantitative credit controls. Ceilings on refinanced crop credits abused and excessive government guarantees contributed to overborrowing by public enterprises.	Flexible interest rate and credit policies adopted. Supervisory and regulatory capacity of central bank reinforced. The banking sector was restructured, several public sector banks were closed and there was a significant reduction in government ownership in others. Since August 1994, the process of securitizing the banking system debt assumed by the Government has been under way.	Real lending interest rates turned positive after reforms. Indicators of financial sector development present a mixed picture—the share of private sector credit in total credit has increased but the ratio of broad money to GDP has remained unchanged. Reforms reasonably successful in restricting government intervention in credit allocation and in interest rate determination.
Thailand	Relatively oligopolistic banking system until mid-1980s when foreign banks were allowed. Interest rates subject to controls. Some directed credit allocation. Relatively open external capital account, especially for inflows.	Financial reforms undertaken at various times in response to particular problems. Important steps include (1) measures to increase competition in banking system and develop interbank money market in 1979; (2) strengthening supervisory arrangements in 1983 and 1985; (3) overall ceiling on domestic credit abolished in 1984; and (4) administered rates that were adjusted to take account of inflation coupled with gradual liberalization of deposit rates (1989–92) and lending rates (1992).	Selective credit policies still in effect. Until the liberalization of lending rates in 1992, spread between deposit and lending rates was wide, suggesting the presence of distortions in banking system. Indicators suggest that substantial progress has been made in developing an efficient financial system.

Table 21. Labor Market Characteristics

Country	Bangladesh	Chile	Ghana	India
General:	Highly segmented labor markets. Large role of public sector. Restrictions on retrenchment.	Important reforms took place after 1973. Labor markets relatively flexible following elimination of wage indexation in 1982.	Substantial labor market segmentation. Public sector prominent in formal market, acts as wage leader for private sector.	Substantial labor market segmentation. Formal markets highly regulated through restrictions on retrenchment.
Labor market segmentation: 1. Size of formal sector	1. About 10 percent of labor force.	1. Formal sector is large relative to informal sector.	1. Formal market small relative to informal market. Labor unions powerful in formal market and public sector.	1. Employment in formal sector about 8 percent of total employment.
2. Wages in formal sector	2. Unskilled public sector wage 68 percent above unskilled agricultural wage in same region.			
Minimum wage laws: 1. Coverage	1. Minimum wages for different skill levels and sectors recommended by the National Minimum Wage Board. Reviews are on an ad hoc basis. Applies to 38 sectors.	1. Minimum wages regulations cover all workers.	1. Minimum wages apply mainly to unskilled formal sector workers.	1. Coverage is narrow.
2. Were they important for wage developments? (e.g., ratio of average to minimum wage)	2. No significant impact on market wages (often below market wages). Government unable to enforce minimum wage regulations.	2. Minimum wage growth in 1982–87 fell below average wage growth, and fell in real terms by 40 percent. By early 1990s, real minimum wage returned to 1982 level.	2. Increases in minimum wages contributed to boosting wage incomes between 1984 and 1990.	2. Minimum wages not effectively enforced and no strong impact on other wages. Ratio of average wage to minimum wage: 7:1 for unskilled workers; 3.5:1 for skilled workers.
Job security regulations: 1. Social security and unemployment insurance	1. No unemployment insurance.	1. Unemployment compensation program covering only a small portion of labor force. Emergency unemployment subsidies created so that 50 percent of unemployed received some assistance in 1982–83.	1. No unemployment insurance.	1. No unemployment insurance.
2. Exit and entry laws	2. Retrenchment is restricted. High severance pay that in practice amounts to a minimum of 60 days of wages for each year of service.	2. Liberal. Restrictions on retrenchment eliminated in 1973.	2. Retrenchment is highly restricted in public sector.	2. Stringent job security regulations; in many cases, firms must obtain prior government consent before laying off workers.
Public sector employment: 1. Size	1. Public sector accounts for 50 percent of value added in manufacturing and one third of formal sector employment.	1. Public sector employment amounted to about 9 percent of total employment in 1986.	1. Government employment accounts for two thirds of total formal sector employment; 21 civil servants per 1,000 inhabitants is high by African standards.	1. About 6 percent of total working age population and over 70 percent of formal sector employment.
2. Ratio of public sector to private wages or similar indicator	2. Public sector average wages greater than private sector. Public and private wages highly correlated.	2. Public sector has little influence on private sector wages and employment.	2. Public sector wages and benefits comparable to private sector for most of 1980s, but in 1995 was one and a half times greater (except for business sector). Private sector competitiveness and profitability suffered from the effect of generous public sector pay awards in 1992.	2. Public sector wages appear to exert considerable leverage over private formal sector wages.

Country	Mexico	Morocco	Senegal	Thailand
Incomes policies: 1. Rules and coverage 2. Were they effective?	1. None.	1. From 1973, government regulations provided for backward-looking wage indexation, until eliminated in 1982.	1. None.	1. None, although public wages are de facto partially indexed.
Reforms undertaken during adjustment:	Adjustment programs envisaged little reform; little reform undertaken.	Starting in 1973, legislation enacted that relaxed restrictions on dismissals, diminished union power, and reduced employer share of social security taxes and other nonwage costs. Mandatory wage indexation abolished in 1982.	Civil service reform in second phase of Economic Recovery Program (1987–91) with view to increasing efficiency. But little net retrenchment in overall government employment. Some progress in linking wage increases to productivity and increasing wage differentials. Modest reduction of state enterprise employment.	Minimal changes; mechanisms established to provide additional compensation for layoffs in public enterprises.
General:	Formal labor markets regulated and wages influenced by wage-price pacts.	Formal labor markets highly regulated through well-enforced minimum wage laws, and restrictions on hiring and retrenchment.	Highly regulated formal sector and poor record of reforms.	Labor markets have been generally flexible and less segmented.
Labor market segmentation: 1. Size of formal sector	1. Formal sector substantial; about 70–75 percent of total employment in 1980–85.	1. Wage employment in 1990: 62 percent of the urban labor force and 17 percent of the rural labor force.	1. Modern sector employment (civilservice, industry, finance) 131,000 in 1986.	1. Formal sector about 25 percent of labor force before adjustment phase and 33 percent afterward.
2. Formal sector wages relative to informal sector			2. Wages in informal sector about one third of formal sector.	
Minimum wage laws: 1. Coverage	1. Introduced in 1970 to cover all workers.	1. SMIG covers all nonagricultural employees and SMAG covers all agricultural employees including temporary and seasonal workers. SMIG has been about 50 percent higher than SMAG since 1986.	1. SMIG covers essentially unskilled urban employees.	1. Introduced in 1973 to cover unskilled nonagricultural workers. About 20 percent of labor force.
2. Were they important for wage developments? (e.g., ratio of average to minimum wage)	2. Diminished importance over time. Ratio of average to minimum wage: 1:0.2 in 1984; 1:0.1 in 1990. Some 16 percent of full-time male workers and 66 percent of female workers paid below minimum wages in 1988.	2. The SMIG is strongly correlated with a lag with average formal sector wage; but more than half of firms paid unskilled workers below minimum wages in 1986.	2. In 1986 the average wage of an unskilled worker was about 20 percent higher than the SMIG.	2. Less than one half of unskilled labor being paid the minimum wage. Ratio of average to minimum wage in Bangkok area is 4:1.
Job security regulations: 1. Social security and unemployment insurance	1. Social security schemes cover formal sector and public sector employment.	1. About 20 percent of urban labor force are covered by National Social Security Fund. No unemployment insurance.	1. Nonwage benefits set by fixed rules.	1. Public sector pension and medical care but no private sector arrangements. Tripartite social security scheme began in 1991 for firms with more than 10 employees. No unemployment insurance.
2. Exit and entry laws	2. Severe restrictions on hiring, firing, and reassignment of workers across plants and production lines.	2. Firing workers is highly regulated and often implies costly severance pay.	2. Prior government authorization required for hiring and retrenchment. Controls on use of temporary workers. Collective bargaining at industry level required.	2. Liberal.

Table 21 *(concluded)*

Country	Mexico	Morocco	Senegal	Thailand
Public sector employment:				
1. Size		1. 1980: government employment was 95 percent of the private urban formal sector employment.	1. 1983: civil service—66,310	1. Four percent of labor force.
2. Ratio of public sector to private wages or similar indicator		2. The average wage is higher in public sector than private sector.	2. 1980–85: SMIG (real terms) fell 22 percent; real average earnings of civil service fell 30 percent.	2. Private sector wages greater than public sector. Estimate of differential is (1.5–2):1.
Incomes policies:				
1. Rules and coverage	1. 1987–early 1995: annual wage-price pacts negotiated among large unions, industrial groups and government linking exchange rate action with understandings on wages, employment, and public sector price increases.	1. Law requires adjustment in minimum wages whenever the cost of living index rises by 5 percent; applies to all sectors; adjustments of SMIG are irregular.	1. None.	1. None.
2. Were they effective?	2. Only increases in minimum wages and public sector prices announced; over time wage guidelines became less representative of actual labor remuneration.	2. Not applied.		
Labor reforms undertaken:	Apart from the removal of de facto backward-looking wage indexation, relatively little fundamental reform undertaken.	Apart from laws on firing, most regulations not binding. Adjustment programs envisaged little reform and little reform was undertaken.	1986–87: hiring practices and use of temporary labor partially liberalized, but critical clauses of labor code not modified. 1991: limited public sector reform. 1994: labor code revised to liberalize hiring and firing practices.	Limited.

Sources: Bangladesh: World Bank (1995); Chile: Meller (1992); Ghana: Nowak and others (forthcoming), Roe and Schneider (1992); India: Chopra and others (1995); Morocco: World Bank (1994c); Senegal: Tahari and others (forthcoming).

References

Agarwala, Ramgopal, "Price Distortions and Growth in Developing Countries," World Bank Staff Working Paper No. 575 (Washington: World Bank, July 1983).

Agénor, Pierre-Richard, "The Labor Market and Economic Adjustment," IMF Working Paper No. 95/125 (Washington: International Monetary Fund, November 1995).

———, and Joshua Aizenman, "Macroeconomic Adjustment with Segmented Labor Markets," NBER Working Paper No. 4769 (Cambridge, Massachusetts: National Bureau of Economic Research, June 1994).

Anand, Ritu, and Sweder van Wijnbergen, "Inflation and the Financing of Government Expenditure: An Introductory Analysis with an Application to Turkey," *World Bank Economic Review,* Vol. 3 (January 1989), pp. 17–38.

Asilis, Carlos M., and Gian Maria Milesi-Ferreti, "On the Political Sustainability of Economic Reform," IMF Paper on Policy Analysis and Assessment No. 94/3 (Washington: International Monetary Fund, January 1994).

Atje, Raymond, and Boyan Jovanovic, "Stock Markets and Development," *European Economic Review,* Vol. 37 (April 1993), pp. 632–40.

Barro, Robert J., "Economic Growth in a Cross-Section of Countries," NBER Working Paper No. 3120 (Cambridge, Massachusetts: National Bureau of Economic Research, September 1989).

———, and Jong-Wha Lee, "International Comparisons of Educational Attainment," *Journal of Monetary Economics,* Vol. 2 (December 1993), pp. 363–94.

Bennett, Adam, "Behavior of Nominal and Real Interest Rates," in *IMF Conditionality: Experience Under Stand-By and Extended Arrangements, Part II: Background Papers,* ed. by Susan Schadler, IMF Occasional Paper No. 129 (Washington: International Monetary Fund, September 1995).

Bercuson, K., and L. Koenig, *The Recent Surge in Capital Inflows to Three Asian Countries: Causes and Macroeconomic Impact,* South East Asian Central Banks, Occasional Paper No. 15 (Kuala Lumpur, 1993).

Bisat, Amer, R. Barry Johnston, and V. Sundararajan, "Issues in Managing and Sequencing Financial Sector Reforms: Lessons from Experiences in Five Developing Countries," IMF Working Paper No. 92/82 (Washington: International Monetary Fund, October 1992).

Boone, Peter, "The Impact of Foreign Aid on Savings and Growth," Working Paper No. 1265 (London: Center for Economic Performance, London School of Economics, November 1994).

Borensztein, Eduardo, Jose De Gregorio, and Jong-Wha Lee, "How Does Foreign Direct Investment Affect Economic Growth?" NBER Working Paper No. 5057 (Cambridge, Massachusetts: National Bureau of Economic Research, March 1995).

Bosworth, Barry P., Rudiger Dornbusch, and Raul Labán, eds., *The Chilean Economy: Policy Lessons and Challenges* (Washington: Brookings Institution, 1994).

Bourguignon, François, and Christian Morrisson, *Adjustment and Equity in Developing Countries: A New Approach* (Paris: Development Center, Organization for Economic Cooperation and Development, 1992).

Branson, William H., and Carl Jayarajah, "A Framework for Evaluating Policy Adjustment Programs: Lessons from a Cross-Country Evaluation," in *Evaluation and Development: Proceedings of the 1994 World Bank Conference* (Washington: World Bank, Operations Evaluation Department, 1995).

Bruno, Michael, S. Fischer, E. Helpman, and N. Liviatan, eds., *Lessons of Economic Stabilization and Its Aftermath* (Cambridge, Massachusetts: MIT Press, 1991).

Bruno, Michael, and William Easterly, "Inflation Crises and Long-Run Growth," NBER Working Paper No. 5209 (Cambridge, Massachusetts: National Bureau of Economic Research, July 1995).

Calvo, Guillermo, and Carlos A. Végh, "Inflation Stabilization and Nominal Anchors," IMF Paper on Policy Analysis and Assessment No. 92/4 (Washington: International Monetary Fund, December 1992).

———, "Exchange-Rate-Based Stabilization Under Imperfect Credibility," in *Open-Economy Macroeconomics,* ed. by Helmut Frisch and Andreas Wörgötter (Houndsmill, Basingstoke, England: Macmillan Press, 1993).

Chhibber, Ajay, Mansoor Dailami, and Nemat Shafik, eds., *Reviving Private Investment in Developing Countries: Empirical Studies and Policy Lessons* (Amsterdam, New York: North-Holland, 1992).

Chopra, Ajay, Charles Collyns, Richard Hemming, and Karen Parker, *India: Economic Reform and Growth,* IMF Occasional Paper No. 134 (Washington: International Monetary Fund, December 1995).

Citrin, Daniel A., and Ashok K. Lahiri, eds., *Policy Experiences and Issues in the Baltics, Russia, and Other Countries of the Former Soviet Union,* IMF Occasional Paper No. 133 (Washington: International Monetary Fund, December 1995).

Claessens, Stijn, Daniel Oks, and Sweder van Wijnbergen, "Interest Rates, Growth and External Debt: The Macroeconomic Impact of Mexico's Brady Deal," CEPR Discussion Paper No. 904 (London: Center for Economic Policy Research, 1994).

Conway, Patrick, "IMF Lending Programs: Participation and Impact," *Journal of Development Economics,* Vol. 45 (December 1994), pp. 365–91.

Corbo, Vittorio, and Klaus Schmidt-Hebbel, "Public Policy and Saving in Developing Countries," *Journal of Development Economics,* Vol. 36 (July 1991), pp. 89–115.

Corbo, Vittorio, Stanley Fischer, and Steven B. Webb, eds., *Adjustment Lending Revisited: Policies to Restore Growth* (Washington: World Bank, 1992).

Currie, Janet, and Ann Harrison, "Trade Reforms and Labor Market Adjustment in Morocco," Labor Markets Workshop (Washington: World Bank, June 1994).

De Gregorio, Jose, "Economic Growth in Latin America," *Journal of Development Economics,* Vol. 39 (July 1992), pp. 59–84.

Dixit, Avinash K., "Investment and Hysteresis," *Journal of Economic Perspectives,* Vol. 6, No. 1 (Winter 1992), pp. 107–32.

———, and Robert S. Pindyck, *Investment Under Uncertainty* (Princeton, New Jersey: Princeton University Press, 1994).

Dornbusch, Rudiger, and Stanley Fischer, "Moderate Inflation," *World Bank Economic Review,* Vol. 7 (January 1993), pp. 1–44.

Easterly, W., "Endogenous Growth in Developing Countries with Government-Induced Distortions," in *Adjustment Lending Revisited: Policies to Restore Growth,* ed. by Vittorio Corbo, Stanley Fischer, and Steven B. Webb (Washington: World Bank, 1992).

———, Carlos A. Rodríguez, and Klaus Schmidt-Hebbel, eds., *Public Sector Deficits and Macroeconomic Performance* (New York: Oxford University Press, 1994).

Edwards, Sebastian, "On the Sequencing of Structural Reforms," NBER Working Paper No. 3138 (Cambridge, Massachusetts: National Bureau of Economic Research, October 1989).

———, "Exchange Rates, Inflation and Disinflation: Latin American Experiences," NBER Working Paper No. 4320 (Cambridge, Massachusetts: National Bureau of Economic Research, April 1993).

Elías, Victor J., *Sources of Growth: A Study of Seven Latin American Countries,* International Center for Economic Growth (San Francisco: ICS Press, 1992).

Faruqee, Hamid, and Aasim M. Husain, "Saving Trends in Southeast Asia: A Cross-Country Analysis," IMF Working Paper No. 95/39 (Washington: International Monetary Fund, April 1995).

Feliciano, M., "Workers and Trade Liberalization: The Impact of Trade Reforms in Mexico on Wages and Employment" (unpublished; Cambridge, Massachusetts: Harvard University, 1994).

Fischer, Stanley, "Role of Macroeconomic Factors in Growth," *Journal of Monetary Economics,* Vol. 32 (December 1993), pp. 485–512.

Hadjimichael, Michael T., Dhaneshwar Ghura, Martin Mühleisen, Roger Nord, and E. Murat Uçer, *Sub-Saharan Africa: Growth, Savings, and Investment, 1986–93,* IMF Occasional Paper No. 118 (Washington: International Monetary Fund, January 1995).

Hadjimichael, Michael T., and Dhaneshwar Ghura, "Public Policies and Private Savings and Investment in Sub-Saharan Africa: An Empirical Investigation," IMF Working Paper No. 95/19 (Washington: International Monetary Fund, February 1995).

Haque, Nadeem U., Kajal Lahiri, and Peter J. Montiel, "Macroeconometric Model for Developing Countries," *Staff Papers,* International Monetary Fund, Vol. 37 (September 1990), pp. 537–59.

Haque, Nadeem U., and Peter J. Montiel, "Dynamic Responses to Policy and Exogenous Shocks in an Empirical Developing Model with Rational Expectations," in *Macroeconomic Models for Adjustment in Developing Countries,* ed. by Mohsin S. Khan, Peter J. Montiel, and Nadeem U. Haque (Washington: International Monetary Fund, 1991).

Horton, Susan, Ravi Kanbur, and Dipak Mazumdar, eds., *Labor Markets in an Era of Adjustment,* Issues Papers, Vols. 1 and 2, EDI Development Studies (Washington: World Bank, 1994).

Husain, Ishrat, and Rashid Faruqee, eds., *Adjustment in Africa: Lessons from Country Case Studies,* World Bank Regional and Sectoral Studies (Washington: World Bank, 1994).

International Monetary Fund, "The Experience of Successfully Adjusting Developing Countries," in *World Economic Outlook, October 1992: A Survey by the Staff of the International Monetary Fund,* World Economic and Financial Surveys (Washington: International Monetary Fund, October 1992).

——— (1993a), "Convergence and Divergence in Developing Countries," in *World Economic Outlook, May 1993: A Survey by the Staff of the International Monetary Fund,* World Economic and Financial Surveys (Washington: International Monetary Fund, May 1993).

——— (1993b), "Domestic and Foreign Saving in Developing Countries," in *World Economic Outlook, October 1993: A Survey by the Staff of the International Monetary Fund,* World Economic and Financial Surveys (Washington: International Monetary Fund, October 1993).

———, "Why Are Some Developing Countries Failing to Catch Up?" in *World Economic Outlook, May 1994: A Survey by the Staff of the International Monetary Fund,* World Economic and Financial Surveys (Washington: International Monetary Fund, May 1994).

———, *World Economic Outlook, May 1995: A Survey by the Staff of the International Monetary Fund,* World Economic and Financial Surveys (Washington: International Monetary Fund, May 1995).

———, Fiscal Affairs Department, *Unproductive Public Expenditures: A Pragmatic Approach to Policy Analysis,* IMF Pamphlet Series, No. 48 (Washington: International Monetary Fund, 1995).

Khan, Mohsin S., "Macroeconomic Effects of Fund-Supported Programs," *Staff Papers,* International Monetary Fund, Vol. 37 (June 1990), pp. 195–221.

———, and Malcolm D. Knight, *Fund-Supported Adjustment Programs and Economic Growth,* IMF Occasional Paper No. 41 (Washington: International Monetary Fund, 1985).

Khan, Mohsin S., and Carmen M. Reinhart, *Capital Flows in the APEC Region,* IMF Occasional Paper No. 122 (Washington: International Monetary Fund, March 1995).

Khan, Mohsin S., Peter J. Montiel, and Nadeem U. Haque, eds., *Macroeconomic Models for Adjustment in Developing Countries* (Washington: International Monetary Fund, 1991).

Kiguel, Miguel A., and Nissan Liviatan, "Business Cycle Associated with Exchange Rate-Based Stabilizations," *World Bank Economic Review,* Vol. 6 (May 1992), pp. 279–305.

King, Robert G., and Ross Levine, "Financial Indicators and Growth in a Cross Section of Countries," Policy Research Working Paper WPS/819 (Washington: World Bank, 1992).

———, "Finance and Growth: Schumpeter Might Be Right," *Quarterly Journal of Economics,* Vol. 108 (August 1993), pp. 717–37.

———, "Capital Fundamentalism, Economic Development, and Economic Growth," *Carnegie-Rochester Conference Series on Public Policy,* Vol. 40 (1994), pp. 259–300.

Kirmani, Naheed, and others, *International Trade Policies: The Uruguay Round and Beyond,* Vols. I and II, World Economic and Financial Surveys (Washington: International Monetary Fund, 1994).

Kochhar, K., L. Dicks-Mireaux, B. Horvath, M. Mecagni, E. Offerdal, and J. Zhou, *Thailand: The Road to Sustained Growth,* International Monetary Fund (forthcoming).

Kormendi, Roger C., and Philip G. Meguire, "Macroeconomic Determinants of Growth: Cross-Country Evidence," *Journal of Monetary Economics,* Vol. 16 (September 1985), pp. 141–63.

Krueger, Anne O., Maurice W. Schiff, and Alberto Valdés, *The Political Economy of Agricultural Pricing Policy* (Baltimore: Johns Hopkins University Press, 1992).

Levine, Ross, and David Renelt, "A Sensitivity Analysis of Cross-Country Growth Regressions," *American Economic Review,* Vol. 82 (September 1992), pp. 942–63.

Little, Ian M.D., R.N. Cooper, W. Corden, and S. Rajapatirana, *Boom, Crisis, and Adjustment: The Macroeconomic Experience of Developing Countries* (New York: Oxford University Press, 1993).

Loser, Claudio M., and Eliot Kalter, eds., *Mexico: The Strategy to Achieve Sustained Economic Growth,* IMF Occasional Paper No. 99 (Washington: International Monetary Fund, 1992).

Mackenzie, George A., and others, *Composition of Fiscal Adjustment and Growth,* International Monetary Fund, (forthcoming).

Mankiw, N. Gregory, David Romer, and David N. Weil, "A Contribution to the Empirics of Economic Growth," *Quarterly Journal of Economics,* Vol. 107 (May 1992), pp. 407–37.

Mariano, Roberto S., "Analytical Small-Sample Distribution Theory in Econometrics: The Simultaneous-Equations Case," *International Economic Review,* Vol. 23 (October 1982), pp. 503–33.

Masson, Paul R., Tamim Bayoumi, and Hossein Samiei, "Saving Behavior in Industrial and Developing Countries," in *Staff Studies for the World Economic Outlook,* by the Research Department of the International Monetary Fund, World Economic and Financial Surveys (Washington: International Moneary Fund, September 1995).

McCarthy, F. Desmond, J. Peter Neary, and Giovanni Zanalda, "Measuring the Effect of External Shocks and the Policy Response to Them: Empirical Methodology Applied to the Philippines," Policy Research Working Paper No. 1271 (Washington: World Bank, March 1994).

Mecagni, Mauro, "Experience with Nominal Anchors," in *IMF Conditionality: Experience Under Stand-By and Extended Arrangements, Part II: Background Papers,* ed. by Susan Schadler, IMF Occasional Paper No. 129 (Washington: International Monetary Fund, September 1995).

Meller, Patricio, *Adjustment and Equity in Chile* (Paris: Development Center of the Organization for Economic Cooperation and Development, 1992).

Montiel, Peter J., "The Transmission Mechanism for Monetary Policy in Developing Countries," *Staff Papers,* International Monetary Fund, Vol. 38 (March 1991), pp. 83–108.

———, "A Macroeconomic Simulation Model for India" (unpublished; Oberlin College, February 1993).

Mosley, Paul, Jane Harrigan, and John Toye, *Aid and Power: The World Bank and Policy-Based Lending* (London: Routledge, 1991; 2nd ed., 1995).

Nehru, Vikram, and A. Dhareshwar, "A New Database on Physical Capital Stock: Sources, Methodology and Results," *Revista de Análisis Económico,* Vol. 8, No. 1 (1993), pp. 37–59.

Nowak, M., R. Basanti, B. Horvath, K. Kochhar, and R. Prem, "Ghana, 1983–91," in *Adjustment for Growth: The African Experience*, International Monetary Fund (forthcoming).

Nsouli, Saleh M., Sena Eken, Klaus Enders, Van-Can Thai, Jörg Decressin, and Filippo Cartiglia, *Resilience and Growth Through Sustained Adjustment: The Moroccan Experience,* IMF Occasional Paper No. 117 (Washington: International Monetary Fund, January 1995).

Ogaki, Masao, Jonathan D. Ostry, and Carmen M. Reinhart, "Saving Behavior in Low- and Middle-Income Developing Countries: A Comparison," *Staff Papers*, International Monetary Fund, Vol. 43 (March 1966), pp. 38–71.

Oks, Daniel, and E. Luttmer, "Mexico: Reform and Productivity Growth," World Bank Report No. 11823-ME (Washington: World Bank, May 1994).

Papageorgiou, Demetrios, Armeane M. Choksi, and Michael Michaely, *Liberalizing Foreign Trade in De-*

veloping Countries: The Lessons of Experience (Washington: World Bank, 1990).

Phillips, P.C.B., "Exact Small Sample Theory in the Simultaneous Equation Model," in *Handbook of Econometrics,* Vol. I, ed. by Zvi Griliches and Michael D. Intrilligator (Amsterdam: North-Holland, 1983).

Pindyck, Robert S., "Irreversibility, Uncertainty and Investment," *Journal of Economic Literature,* Vol. 29 (September 1991), pp. 1110–49.

Rebelo, Sergio, and Carlos A. Végh, "Real Effects of Exchange-Rate-Based Stabilization: An Analysis of Competing Theories," in *NBER Macroeconomics Annual, 1995* (Cambridge, Massachusetts: MIT Press, 1995).

Reinhart, Carmen M., and Carlos A. Végh, "Nominal Interest Rates, Consumption Booms, and Lack of Credibility: A Quantitative Examination," *Journal of Development Economics,* Vol. 46 (April 1995), pp. 357–78.

Revenga, Ana, "Employment and Wage Effects of Trade Liberalization: The Case of Mexican Manufacturing," Policy Research Working Paper No. 1524 (Washington: World Bank, 1995).

Roe, Alan, and Hartmut Schneider, *Adjustment and Equity in Ghana* (Paris: Development Center of the Organization for Economic Cooperation and Development, 1992).

Sachs, J., "Wages, Profits and Macroeconomic Adjustment: A Comparative Study," *Brookings Papers on Economic Activity* (2/1979), pp. 269–332.

Sarel, Michael, "Demographic Dynamics and the Empirics of Economic Growth," *Staff Papers,* International Monetary Fund, Vol. 42 (June 1995), pp. 398–410.

———, "Nonlinear Effects of Inflation on Economic Growth," *Staff Papers*, International Monetary Fund, Vol. 43 (March 1996), pp. 199–215.

Savastano, Miguel A., "Private Saving in IMF Arrangements," in *IMF Conditionality: Experience Under Stand-By and Extended Arrangements, Part II: Background Papers,* ed. by Susan Schadler, IMF Occasional Paper No. 129 (Washington: International Monetary Fund, September 1995).

Schadler, Susan, Franek Rozwadowski, Siddharth Tiwari, and David O. Robinson, *Economic Adjustment in Low-Income Countries: Experience Under the Enhanced Structural Adjustment Facility,* IMF Occasional Paper No. 106 (Washington: International Monetary Fund, September 1993).

Schadler, Susan, Maria Carkovic, Adam Bennett, and Robert Kahn, *Recent Experiences with Surges in Capital Inflows,* IMF Occasional Paper No. 108 (Washington: International Monetary Fund, December 1993).

Schadler, Susan, Adam Bennett, Maria Carkovic, Louis Dicks-Mireaux, Mauro Mecagni, James H.J. Morsink, and Miguel A. Savastano, *IMF Conditionality: Experience Under Stand-By and Extended Arrangements, Part I: Key Issues and Findings,* IMF Occasional Paper No. 128 (Washington: International Monetary Fund, September 1995).

Schadler, Susan, ed., *IMF Conditionality: Experience Under Stand-By and Extended Arrangements, Part II: Background Papers,* IMF Occasional Paper No. 129 (Washington: International Monetary Fund, September 1995).

Schmidt-Hebbel, Klaus, and Steven B. Webb, "Public Policy and Private Saving," in *Adjustment Lending Revisited: Policies to Restore Growth,* ed. by Vittorio Corbo, Stanley Fischer, and Steven B. Webb (Washington: World Bank, 1992).

Serven, Luis, and Andrés Solimano, eds., *Striving for Growth After Adjustment: The Role of Capital Formation,* World Bank Regional and Sectoral Studies (Washington: World Bank, 1994).

Tahari, A., J. de Vrijer, and M. Fouad, "Senegal, 1978–93," in *Adjustment for Growth: The African Experience,* International Monetary Fund (forthcoming).

Thomas, Vinod, John D. Nash, and others, *Best Practices in Trade Policy Reform* (New York: Oxford University Press, 1991).

Thomas, Vinod, Ajay Chhibber, M. Dailami, and Jaime de Melo, eds., *Restructuring Economies in Distress: Policy Reform and the World Bank* (New York: Oxford University Press, 1991).

Tinakorn, Pranee, and Chalongphob Sussangkarn, "Productivity Growth in Thailand" (unpublished; Bangkok: National Economic and Social Development Board and Thailand Development Research Institute, 1994).

Woo, Wing Thye, Bruce Glassburner, and Anwar Nasution, *Macroeconomic Policies, Crises, and Long-Term Growth in Indonesia, 1965–90,* World Bank Comparative Macroeconomic Studies (Washington: World Bank, 1994).

World Bank, "Adjustment Lending Policies for Sustainable Growth," Policy and Research Series, No. 14 (Washington: World Bank, 1990).

———, *World Development Report 1991* (New York: Oxford University Press, 1991).

———, "Adjustment Lending and Mobilization of Private and Public Resources for Growth," Policy and Research Series, No. 22 (Washington: World Bank, 1992).

——— (1993a), *Ghana 2000 and Beyond: Setting the Stage for Accelerated Growth and Poverty Reduction* (Washington: World Bank, February 1993).

——— (1993b), *The East Asian Miracle: Economic Growth and Public Policy* (New York: Oxford University Press, 1993).

——— (1994a), *Adjustment in Africa: Reforms, Results, and the Road Ahead* (New York: Oxford University Press, 1994).

——— (1994b), "Mexico: Country Economic Memorandum—Fostering Private Sector Development in the 1990s," Report No. 11823-ME (Washington: World Bank, May 1994).

——— (1994c), "Kingdom of Morocco—Preparing for the 21st Century: Strengthening the Private Sector in Morocco," Report No. 11894-MOR (Washington: World Bank, June 1994).

————, *World Development Report 1995* (New York: Oxford University Press, 1995).

————, Operations Evaluation Department, *Trade Reforms Under Adjustment Programs* (Washington: World Bank, 1992).

————, Operations Evaluation Department, *Structural and Sectoral Adjustment: World Bank Experience, 1980–92* (Washington: World Bank, 1995).

Recent Occasional Papers of the International Monetary Fund

139. Reinvigorating Growth in Developing Countries: Lessons from Adjustment Policies in Eight Economies, by David Goldsbrough, Sharmini Coorey, Louis Dicks-Mireaux, Balazs Horvath, Kalpana Kochhar, Mauro Mecagni, Erik Offerdal, and Jianping Zhou. 1996.

138. Aftermath of the CFA Franc Devaluation, by Jean A.P. Clément, with Johannes Mueller, Stéphane Cossé, and Jean Le Dem. 1996.

137. The Lao People's Democratic Republic: Systemic Transformation and Adjustment, edited by Ichiro Otani and Chi Do Pham. 1996.

136. Jordan: Strategy for Adjustment and Growth, edited by Edouard Maciejewski and Ahsan Mansur. 1996.

135. Vietnam: Transition to a Market Economy, by John R. Dodsworth, Erich Spitäller, Michael Braulke, Keon Hyok Lee, Kenneth Miranda, Christian Mulder, Hisanobu Shishido, and Krishna Srinivasan. 1996.

134. India: Economic Reform and Growth, by Ajai Chopra, Charles Collyns, Richard Hemming, and Karen Parker with Woosik Chu and Oliver Fratzscher. 1995.

133. Policy Experiences and Issues in the Baltics, Russia, and Other Countries of the Former Soviet Union, edited by Daniel A. Citrin and Ashok K. Lahiri. 1995.

132. Financial Fragilities in Latin America: The 1980s and 1990s, by Liliana Rojas-Suárez and Steven R. Weisbrod. 1995.

131. Capital Account Convertibility: Review of Experience and Implications for IMF Policies, by staff teams headed by Peter J. Quirk and Owen Evans. 1995.

130. Challenges to the Swedish Welfare State, by Desmond Lachman, Adam Bennett, John H. Green, Robert Hagemann, and Ramana Ramaswamy. 1995.

129. IMF Conditionality: Experience Under Stand-By and Extended Arrangements. Part II: Background Papers. Susan Schadler, Editor, with Adam Bennett, Maria Carkovic, Louis Dicks-Mireaux, Mauro Mecagni, James H.J. Morsink, and Miguel A. Savastano. 1995.

128. IMF Conditionality: Experience Under Stand-By and Extended Arrangements. Part I: Key Issues and Findings, by Susan Schadler, Adam Bennett, Maria Carkovic, Louis Dicks-Mireaux, Mauro Mecagni, James H.J. Morsink, and Miguel A. Savastano. 1995.

127. Road Maps of the Transition: The Baltics, the Czech Republic, Hungary, and Russia, by Biswajit Banerjee, Vincent Koen, Thomas Krueger, Mark S. Lutz, Michael Marrese, and Tapio O. Saavalainen. 1995.

126. The Adoption of Indirect Instruments of Monetary Policy, by a Staff Team headed by William E. Alexander, Tomás J.T. Baliño, and Charles Enoch. 1995.

125. United Germany: The First Five Years—Performance and Policy Issues, by Robert Corker, Robert A. Feldman, Karl Habermeier, Hari Vittas, and Tessa van der Willigen. 1995.

124. Saving Behavior and the Asset Price "Bubble" in Japan: Analytical Studies, edited by Ulrich Baumgartner and Guy Meredith. 1995.

123. Comprehensive Tax Reform: The Colombian Experience, edited by Parthasarathi Shome. 1995.

122. Capital Flows in the APEC Region, edited by Mohsin S. Khan and Carmen M. Reinhart. 1995.

121. Uganda: Adjustment with Growth, 1987–94, by Robert L. Sharer, Hema R. De Zoysa, and Calvin A. McDonald. 1995.

120. Economic Dislocation and Recovery in Lebanon, by Sena Eken, Paul Cashin, S. Nuri Erbas, Jose Martelino, and Adnan Mazarei. 1995.

119. Singapore: A Case Study in Rapid Development, edited by Kenneth Bercuson with a staff team comprising Robert G. Carling, Aasim M. Husain, Thomas Rumbaugh, and Rachel van Elkan. 1995.

118. Sub-Saharan Africa: Growth, Savings, and Investment, by Michael T. Hadjimichael, Dhaneshwar Ghura, Martin Mühleisen, Roger Nord, and E. Murat Uçer. 1995.

117. Resilience and Growth Through Sustained Adjustment: The Moroccan Experience, by Saleh M. Nsouli, Sena Eken, Klaus Enders, Van-Can Thai, Jörg Decressin, and Filippo Cartiglia, with Janet Bungay. 1995.

116. Improving the International Monetary System: Constraints and Possibilities, by Michael Mussa, Morris Goldstein, Peter B. Clark, Donald J. Mathieson, and Tamim Bayoumi. 1994.

115. Exchange Rates and Economic Fundamentals: A Framework for Analysis, by Peter B. Clark, Leonardo Bartolini, Tamim Bayoumi, and Steven Symansky. 1994.

114. Economic Reform in China: A New Phase, by Wanda Tseng, Hoe Ee Khor, Kalpana Kochhar, Dubravko Mihaljek, and David Burton. 1994.

113. Poland: The Path to a Market Economy, by Liam P. Ebrill, Ajai Chopra, Charalambos Christofides, Paul Mylonas, Inci Otker, and Gerd Schwartz. 1994.

112. The Behavior of Non-Oil Commodity Prices, by Eduardo Borensztein, Mohsin S. Khan, Carmen M. Reinhart, and Peter Wickham. 1994.

111. The Russian Federation in Transition: External Developments, by Benedicte Vibe Christensen. 1994.

110. Limiting Central Bank Credit to the Government: Theory and Practice, by Carlo Cottarelli. 1993.

109. The Path to Convertibility and Growth: The Tunisian Experience, by Saleh M. Nsouli, Sena Eken, Paul Duran, Gerwin Bell, and Zühtü Yücelik. 1993.

108. Recent Experiences with Surges in Capital Inflows, by Susan Schadler, Maria Carkovic, Adam Bennett, and Robert Kahn. 1993.

107. China at the Threshold of a Market Economy, by Michael W. Bell, Hoe Ee Khor, and Kalpana Kochhar with Jun Ma, Simon N'guiamba, and Rajiv Lall. 1993.

106. Economic Adjustment in Low-Income Countries: Experience Under the Enhanced Structural Adjustment Facility, by Susan Schadler, Franek Rozwadowski, Siddharth Tiwari, and David O. Robinson. 1993.

105. The Structure and Operation of the World Gold Market, by Gary O'Callaghan. 1993.

104. Price Liberalization in Russia: Behavior of Prices, Household Incomes, and Consumption During the First Year, by Vincent Koen and Steven Phillips. 1993.

103. Liberalization of the Capital Account: Experiences and Issues, by Donald J. Mathieson and Liliana Rojas-Suárez. 1993.

102. Financial Sector Reforms and Exchange Arrangements in Eastern Europe. Part I: Financial Markets and Intermediation, by Guillermo A. Calvo and Manmohan S. Kumar. Part II: Exchange Arrangements of Previously Centrally Planned Economies, by Eduardo Borensztein and Paul R. Masson. 1993.

101. Spain: Converging with the European Community, by Michel Galy, Gonzalo Pastor, and Thierry Pujol. 1993.

100. The Gambia: Economic Adjustment in a Small Open Economy, by Michael T. Hadjimichael, Thomas Rumbaugh, and Eric Verreydt. 1992.

99. Mexico: The Strategy to Achieve Sustained Economic Growth, edited by Claudio Loser and Eliot Kalter. 1992.

98. Albania: From Isolation Toward Reform, by Mario I. Blejer, Mauro Mecagni, Ratna Sahay, Richard Hides, Barry Johnston, Piroska Nagy, and Roy Pepper. 1992.

97. Rules and Discretion in International Economic Policy, by Manuel Guitián. 1992.

96. Policy Issues in the Evolving International Monetary System, by Morris Goldstein, Peter Isard, Paul R. Masson, and Mark P. Taylor. 1992.

95. The Fiscal Dimensions of Adjustment in Low-Income Countries, by Karim Nashashibi, Sanjeev Gupta, Claire Liuksila, Henri Lorie, and Walter Mahler. 1992. 94. Tax Harmonization in the European Community: Policy Issues and Analysis, edited by George Kopits. 1992.

Note: For information on the title and availability of Occasional Papers not listed, please consult the IMF Publications Catalog or contact IMF Publication Services.